Acclaim for David Rock and *Quiet Leadership*

"*Quiet Leadership* will help you improve other people's *thinking,* which is the best place to begin improving performance."
—Marshall Goldsmith, founder of Marshall Goldsmith Partners; named one of the fifty great thinkers and leaders who have impacted the field of management by the American Management Association

"Rock has broken the code on how to leverage our most basic human function— thinking! He brings both art and science to the necessary steps for leaders to fol- low in elevating the thinking of their employees in support of world-class performance. Both practical and profound—a must read for anyone who wants to unleash the the potential of their team!"
—Michael W. Morrison, Dean, University of Toyota

"In the first major book to explore what business leaders ought to know about the brain, David Rock creatively marshals an abundance of new research to coherently explain how it advances the use of mind-based brain change as the dynamic ele- ment of better leadership training. *The key to the future of leadership development lies in these pages.*"
—Jeffrey Schwartz, MD, author of *The Mind & The Brain* and *Brain Lock*

"Success depends on the quality of thinking. In the past, if we wanted to change our habitual forms of thinking, we operated in the dark—because nobody had taken the cutting-edge insights of neuroscientists and rephrased them in ordinary language or a business context. Now David Rock has done exactly that, and done it well."
—Art Kleiner, editor in chief, *Strategy+Business* magazine

"One of the most innovative and practical contributions to building effective coaching capability in leaders."
—Joe Bonito, vice president, Global Leadership Effectiveness, Pfizer, Inc.

Quiet
LEADERSHIP

Six Steps to Transforming
Performance at Work

Quiet
LEADERSHIP

Help People Think Better—
Don't Tell Them What to Do!

DAVID ROCK

Collins
An Imprint of HarperCollinsPublishers

HarperCollins books may be purchased for educational, business, or sales promotional use. For information, please write: Special Markets Department, HarperCollins Publishers, 10 East 53rd Street, New York, NY 10022.

FIRST EDITION

Designed by Joy O'Meara

Library of Congress Cataloging-in-Publication Data has been applied for.

ISBN-13: 978-0-06-083590-3
ISBN-10: 0-06-083590-7

06 07 08 09 10 DIX/RRD 10 9 8 7 6 5 4 3 2 1

CONTENTS

■ Part Three ■
Putting the Six Steps to Use   187

ACKNOWLEDGMENTS

There is a woman at the beginning of all great things.

ALPHONSE DE LAMARTINE (1790–1869)

This book would not exist without the love, support, and belief of my wife, Lisa. Since the day we met she's encouraged me to follow my passion and work out how to make a living from it, rather than the other way around, and then stuck by me through good times and bad. Lisa, thank you for your patience and support—you're my rock. Also thanks to my daughter Trinity, whose love of every moment keeps me sane each day. Reading is her favorite pastime; hopefully she'll enjoy this book one day too.

A big thanks to everyone at Results Coaching Systems who put up with a sometimes-overloaded CEO while I squeezed in writing this book. Interacting with some of the best coaches in the world is an honor and privilege. Thanks for your ongoing commitment to making the world a better place by improving people's ability to coach others.

A big thanks to my researcher and chief scientist, Marisa Galisteo, PhD, for a tremendous job keeping me accurate and thorough, and for her passion for the nexus between leadership and neuroscience. Also thanks to everyone who volunteered to be part of my coaching research group, for your dedication to improving our understanding of what it takes to create change in others.

A big warm thanks to my friend and mentor Alexander Caillet, for your guidance and wisdom over the years, and to Ken Manning for the same. I learned so much from both of you. Also thanks to Jeffrey M. Schwartz, M.D., for taking me under your scientific wing recently and sharing everything you know. And thanks to so many scientists and great thinkers, who I have studied from afar, for paving the way for breakthroughs in how we improve our world, including Dr. Martin Seligman, Dr. Mihali Csikszentmihalyi, Edward De Bono, Theodore Zeldin, Mark Jung-Beeman, and many others. Thanks to the many reviewers who gave me honest and thorough feedback about the book during development. Thanks to Karen-Jane Eyre, for your regular support and feedback over the development of the whole book. And finally, thanks to Brian Murray, Herb Schaffner, Marion Maneker, Joe Tessitore, and the rest of the people at Collins for their belief in me.

INTRODUCTION

*When will the way we relate to each other catch up
with developments in technology?*

THEODORE ZELDIN (2003)

In 2004 I met with a large technology company in Singapore that
was desperate to understand how to improve its people's performance. A woman named Anna who headed up the learning and development team took me on a tour of the group's purpose-built
operations center. While wandering through their offices, Anna
pointed out remnants of various performance improvement initia-
tives they'd rolled out over the last few years. They had been trying to
improve the performance of their call center and reduce a crippling
40 percent turnover rate of employees.

Four years ago, consultants told them the problem was no one
could define good performance. So the organization invested substantial resources into identifying some performance indicators.
They decided to track three things: the number of seconds until a call
was picked up; how many calls were picked up under sixty seconds;
and the number of calls that hung up before being answered. They
began sharing this data widely at monthly meetings, yet this made no
difference to performance, and had no impact on retention.

The next year, new consultants declared the problem was a lack of immediate feedback about performance; getting data at the end of the month was too late. This seemed logical to the organization, and further resources were invested so that everyone could get real-time feedback from live screens. This time they got a slight improvement in performance, though they couldn't tell if this was from the screens or other factors. However there was no improvement in retention, an area still costing them dearly.

The following year, someone in management felt they could pinpoint the problem better by surveying their staff. An extensive cultural audit showed that people didn't feel appreciated by their managers or by the organization. So the investment that year was in a reward and recognition program. Anna pointed out a wall twelve feet high and twenty feet long, filled with various monthly awards. Again management found no impact on performance, and no impact on retention.

I asked Anna what she was thinking of doing next. "Our people say they don't know what's expected of them, and they don't feel appreciated. Yet we've addressed these things already," she exclaimed. "What else can we possibly do?"

Looking around their offices, I saw several managers leaning over people's shoulders giving rapid instructions. In the distance I saw training under way in a glass-walled room, most of the participants nodding off. "Have you thought about changing the way your leaders and managers speak to their people?" I asked. "How can we change the way leaders lead, when we can't change anyone else's behavior?" she replied. "Well," I said, "it sounds like you might need to take a whole new approach."

This book outlines that new approach to leadership. It's for busy leaders, executives, and managers who want to improve their employees' performance, and are ready to try something new. It's for the CEO who wants to be more effective at inspiring high-quality thinking in his or her leadership team, but has just a few minutes each week to speak to them. It's for the executive who'd like to get a manager to plan more effectively, but can't seem to work out how. It's for the manager who wants to inspire their sales team, but isn't sure how to do it. And it's for the human resources professional who is ready to take on changing the culture of a whole organization.

The new approach is what I call "Quiet Leadership." Quiet Leaders are masters at bringing out the best performance in others. They improve their employees' thinking—literally improving the way their brains process information—without telling anyone what to do. Given how many people in today's companies are being paid to think, improving thinking is one of the fastest ways to improve performance.

Quiet Leadership is not an academic theory; instead, it's a practical, six-step guide to a new way of having conversations, based on recent discoveries about how the brain works. The central part of this book, the Six Steps to Transforming Performance, points to a new way of thinking, a new way of listening, a new way of speaking, a new approach to every conversation a leader has with their people.

The Six Steps to Transforming Performance were developed over ten years, through designing and delivering workshops to more than five thousand professionals across the United States, the United Kingdom, South Africa, Singapore, Hong Kong, Australia, and New Zealand. At first, these workshops were about how to be a more effective performance coach. In time I saw that coaching was such a central foundation of leadership. From that point on, my focus became developing great leaders by improving their ability to bring out the best performance in others.

My approach has always been scientific and process-focused: I wanted to deconstruct the "code" behind those high-impact conversations that transformed people's performance. Over years of thinking about this issue, identifying patterns, testing out models, and then refining everything further, I developed a set of ideas that was transforming people's ability to impact others. The Six Steps represent the most important ideas that came out of this decade-long process. Some people say I have done for performance coaching what Six Sigma did for the concept of quality: process-mapping best practice, thereby making it more of a science.

A few years ago I started to see strong links between what I had developed and what was now coming out of neuroscience. I found I could describe what I had created based on new findings about the brain, and I began the journey of integrating an understanding of the brain into my approach. This made the ideas even more effective, and opened the door to working at higher levels in organizations, teaching these models to dozens of large corporations, including four Fortune 100 clients. Then in 2004, after working with more than one thousand leaders inside large organizations, I felt ready to put everything into a book.

I have found that the Six Steps are useful at every organizational level: from enabling CEOs to better develop their successors, to helping senior executives become more effective leaders of their general managers, down to line managers becoming better leaders of frontline staff. The Six Steps have helped leaders from many industry sectors, including financial services, information technology, manufacturing, airlines, health care, and government. While I wrote this book primarily for leaders and managers, the ideas here are relevant to teaching, training, coaching, mentoring, counseling, even parenting: any situation where an individual wants to improve another person's performance or facilitate any kind of change.

The book is broken down into three parts. Part one gives you some context for the book and the background theory behind the Six Steps. We start with an introductory chapter, "Why Should Leaders Care About Improving Thinking?" Here we identify the key workplace trends that provide the setting for this book. Next we dive into the workings of the brain in "Recent Discoveries About the Brain that Change Everything," exploring the discoveries that shine a light on this new approach to leadership. This chapter provides a broad theoretical base for why and how the ideas in this book work, and explains why much of our current approach usually doesn't.

Part two is all about the Six Steps. The first of the Six Steps is to learn to "Think About Thinking." This is followed by a new way to listen, "Listen for Potential." Step Three is about a new way of approaching every conversation, "Speak with Intent." I have included some insights here on how to improve the way we communicate by email, an area of significant pain for most employees today. In Step Four we "Dance Toward Insight": we explore the first layer of the conversational process map, the mechanics of how we help other people develop insights. We also learn to recognize what's going on in people's brains by reading their facial expressions, in a model called "The Four Faces of Insight." In Step Five we learn to "Create New Thinking," with the second layer of the process map, called the CREATE model. The CREATE model describes the phases that people go through when real breakthroughs in thinking occur. The last step is called "Follow Up," which is about ensuring that any change we facilitate has the best chance of becoming a long-term habit. Here we use the FEELING model to follow up on the actions people have set for themselves.

Each of the Six Steps contains exercises to help you build new mental muscles. If that's your goal, I recommend reading one chapter a week and doing the exercises as you go. Developing new habits is like eating: You can't eat a week's worth of food in one day and expect to take it all in. I'm not saying you won't get benefits out of reading the book in one sitting; however, working through it slowly will be even more beneficial.

Part three of the book, Putting the Six Steps to Use, is where we see how the Six Steps can be applied to the most common leader-employee interactions. We explore how to help others make better decisions or solve problems. We identify a new model for giving feedback when people have done well, and when they haven't. There's a chapter on using the steps with teams and an additional chapter on how you might use them with children. Finally, I share my thoughts on integrating the Six Steps into an organization's culture at a system-wide level, to bring about that new approach so needed in many workplaces today.

I have tried to make the book as readable as possible, simplifying complex ideas by using metaphor and analogy, and creating illustrations where I can. There are also some extra online resources at www .quietleadership.com, including additional readings and links, as well as online questionnaires I have created to gather data for research purposes. I have intentionally left out the detailed science in the body of the text, giving you references if you want to go deeper. If the book gets to be heavy going at any point, try jumping to part three to see the models being used in context. At the back of the book is a glossary of scientific terms and the models I introduce—you may find this a handy reference.

When I first introduce these ideas to leaders, one of their common concerns is that they don't want to waste time having "unnecessary conversations" with their teams. However, it's been my experience that applying the Six Steps to Transforming Performance will, in most instances, result in leaders having *fewer* conversations over time, not more. And not only that, but their conversations will be shorter, more energizing, and significantly more productive. Many people once introduced to this work realize they waste significant energy when they *don't* apply the Six Steps. One of the biggest inefficiencies in organizations is the conversation that doesn't achieve its intent. Using the Six Steps can make a big difference.

In the last fifty years, our ability to process information via computers has jumped from a mere fourteen bits of information per second, to processing billions of bits per second. Perhaps it's time, as Theodore Zeldin said in my opening quote, for our ability to relate to each other to catch up with our developments in technology. My hope is that this book will go a small way toward helping us all move in this direction.

WHY SHOULD LEADERS CARE ABOUT IMPROVING THINKING?

People don't need to be managed, they need to be unleashed.

RICHARD FLORIDA (2002)

Our leadership practices are not keeping up with the realities of organizational life. The result is an increasing gap between the way employees are being managed at work, and the way they *want* to be managed. Countless surveys have been done in this area, ending in headlines like "Six out of 10 workers are miserable"[1] and "74 percent of staff not engaged at work."[2] Dig into these surveys and you'll see the quality of leadership on top of the list of complaints.

The poor state of leadership and management skills in organizations is being driven by a broad range of factors, including the changing nature of work, the increasing education of employees, the needs of later generations, and the pace of change. Let's explore these concerns.

PAID TO THINK

One hundred years ago most people were paid for their physical labor. The dominant management model was the master-apprentice, and the role of the manager was to improve how people carried out observable physical activities such as hammering and plowing.

By the mid-twentieth century we'd had a big shift in what people were doing for a living, driven by the advent of electricity and mechanization. Much of our work now involved executing codified processes that required less physical exertion. Workers were paid to undertake repetitive tasks: entering data, filing paper, running machinery. The dominant leadership paradigm became the management of processes: scientifically analyzing linear systems to find ever greater efficiencies. The people driving the processes didn't need to be superintelligent, just smart enough to follow plans laid out by management.

In the last few decades, any kind of process work—anything that could be codified or systemized—has been either computerized or outsourced to the lowest-cost country. The number of processes having the people taken out of them is continuing apace, at times with some disturbing consequences. A colleague in recruiting wanted to see how *Fortune* magazine's "100 Best Companies to Work For" treated candidates in their automated recruitment process. He applied online to each company with a made-up CV, perfect in every sense—except the person applying for the job was Goldilocks. Goldilocks received job interest from a frightening number of companies that rely on "intelligent" software to do their initial screening.

By 2005, as a result of all this computerizing, outsourcing, and other process improvements, 40 percent of employees were considered to be knowledge workers.[3] For mid-level management and above, that number is close to 100 percent. So a lot of people in companies are now being paid to think. Yet the management models we're applying to our workforces are still those of the process era. We have not yet taught our leaders and managers how to improve *thinking*. Imagine a factory where artists painted pictures, and the people managing them had not studied how to improve the quality of painting itself, only how to build better canvases and frames.

MANAGING BRILLIANT MINDS

Employees today are better educated than any previous generation. The MBA is now less a mark of distinction and more a requirement for entry. Thirty years ago there were a handful of universities delivering MBAs; now there are thousands. So not only do leaders now need to improve thinking, they need to do so with extremely knowledgeable individuals.

As well as being more educated, employees across the western world have more independence, and on the whole, more wealth. Millions of executives worldwide now enjoy the kind of wealth that only a fraction of the population had fifty years ago. You can't just walk up to a wealthy executive in charge of a $100 million revenue stream and start telling them what to do, just because you are "the boss."

The increasing education and independence of employees is an important issue. Yet we have not significantly reinvented our management models since the times Henry Ford hired a pair of hands and wished they'd left their brains behind.

The Needs of Generations X and Y

The new generations coming into management positions have different needs from their predecessors. These people expect more from an organization. They want to develop personally; they value freedom and independence. They enjoy diversity and change. These people need a different type of leader than our command-and-control cultures have been churning out. They need leaders who help them shine, who help them fulfill their potential at work. Leaders who improve their thinking.

THE PACE OF CHANGE

When today's management models were developed, we lived in a time where product life cycles were ten years. Now life cycles can be ten months, or even ten days, a pace of change that would terrify a

1970s' executive. When a big change initiative comes along, the first job of the leader is to change people's thinking. Again, most leaders have been trained to change processes, not people.

PERFORMANCE IS JUST THE TIP OF THE ICEBERG

There is a metaphor called the Iceberg model used by cognitive behavioral therapy and various behavioral sciences.[4] The Iceberg model describes how our performance at anything is driven by our sets of behaviors, our habits. These are driven by our feelings, which in turn are driven by our thoughts.

In the Iceberg model, our performance and some of our behaviors are visible, while other behaviors, feelings, and thoughts are below the water. There's a lot more driving our performance than just the few habits we see on the surface. And at the base of all this is the way we think.

In other words, what we achieve at work is driven by how we think. Yet when a leader wants to improve someone's performance,

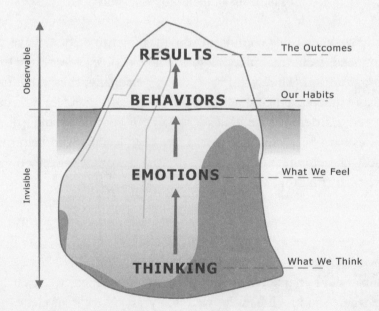

Figure 1, The Iceberg Model

they tend to stay at the surface and focus on the performance itself. They rarely discuss which habits might be driving the employee's performance, or discuss their feelings, and even less often have a conversation about the person's thinking. Yet if you want to improve performance, the most effective way to do this is to start at the bottom—to improve thinking. This might sound complex, yet my experience is that if you focus on just *improving* thinking, rather than trying to understand or unravel it, the conversations are surprisingly quick and simple.

ANSWERING THE LEADERSHIP CRISIS

There is a leadership crisis in many organizations, a lack of the right talent to fill key positions at mid to senior levels. This partly explains executive salaries and the amounts paid to search firms.

The concept of a leadership pipeline, developed by Ram Charan, Stephen Drotter, and James Noel,[5] describes the critical passages that leaders go through, such as moving from managing oneself to managing others. As leaders go through each phase, they also need to change the way they think, yet organizations have scant internal resources allocated to helping people go through this change.

To me, organizations have developed solid pipelines to carry leaders up the mountain, in the form of well-defined sets of competencies and leadership frameworks. They have the contents of the pipes, lower-level leaders. What they are missing is the pumps to drive their leaders to higher levels of effectiveness. They need to instill in their leaders and managers the ability to transform performance by improving thinking.

In summary, it's time leaders learned how to improve people's thinking. Thinking is what many employees are being paid to do, after all. Many employees are highly capable individuals who will thrive on this approach. They want to work smarter, they want to *be* smarter, and they are crying out for help.

Part One

Recent Discoveries About the Brain That Change Everything

*Today's revolutionary advances in neuroscience
will rival the discoveries of Copernicus,
Galileo and Darwin.*

PAUL CHURCHLAND (1996)

Ten years ago I became fascinated by the sealed magic box that is the seat of our thinking, our choices, and our selves. I've now devoured dozens of books and hundreds of articles about how the brain works, from fields including evolutionary psychology, systems theory, genetics, linguistics, and neurophysiology. In 2003 I began to introduce a few concepts about brain functioning into my coaching programs and started to notice strong links between what scientists were finding out about the brain, and how I had been training leaders to be better coaches. I began to see that central to leadership was the ability to improve people's thinking. Therefore leaders might benefit from knowing more about the thing that does the thinking.

Over several years of including a study of the brain in my various classes, a set of core discoveries about the brain emerged. I began to see the central ideas that anyone wanting to understand how to change human behavior should know. These insights trace their origins to brain research by a wide range of neuroscientists including Gerald Edelman, John Ratey, Jeffrey Schwartz, Joseph LeDoux, Michael Merzenich, Edward Taub, Jeff Hawkins, Thomas B. Czerner, and many others. These insights, when fully appreciated, have the power to fundamentally rewrite the rules for nearly every human endeavor involving thinking and learning, including how we educate our children, how we hire and manage staff, how we train people in the workplace, and how we develop leaders.

To me, these insights help explain why therapy often doesn't deliver real change, why trying to give advice is usually futile, why managers are not meeting the needs of workers today, and much, much more. But enough of what *my* brains thinks about all this—let's get into it.

THE BRAIN IS A CONNECTION MACHINE

*Your brain craves patterns and
searches for them endlessly.*

THOMAS B. CZERNER (2001)

Scientists have discovered that our brain is a connection machine. Or to be more specific, the underlying functionality of our brain is one of finding associations, connections, and links between bits of information.[1] Our thoughts, memories, skills, and attributes are vast sets of connections or "maps"[2] joined together via complex chemical and physical pathways. I will call these connections maps from here on as it's a short, memorable word; however you can replace this word with *circuits, wiring,* or *neural pathway* if you prefer.

To give you a sense of the complexity of these maps, imagine a topographic map of one square mile of forest, on a sheet of paper one foot square. Add in the specific details of all the animals living there, from the microbes to major mammals, and the complete specifications of every plant, fungus, and bacteria. Include in the details of each object its size, shape, color, smell, texture, and a history of its interactions with every other object, and then include a snapshot of this information for every moment in time going back forty years. That should give you a sense of how rich these maps are. As it turns out, our brains are made up of maps, and maps of maps, and maps of maps of . . . you get my drift. These sets of maps are created through a process of the brain making over a million new connections every second between different points. Quite something.

So every thought, skill, and attribute we have is a complex map of connections between pieces of information stored in many parts of the brain. For example, the idea of a "car" is a complex, ever changing map of connections between our cognitive or high-level thinking center, our deeper motor skills center where our hardwired activities are held, and many other regions in the brain. The map for car for you might include links to the name and shape of every car you remember, the memory of your driving test including the look of panic on your instructor's face when you nearly sideswiped that truck, the sound of your car when it is running smoothly, your understanding of how an engine works, the history of cars, and even remembering where you left your keys.

Consider what happens when we are trying to think. When we process any new idea we create a map of that idea in our mind, and then compare it subconsciously in a fraction of a second to our existing maps. If we can find solid enough links between the new idea and our current maps, if we can find the connections, we create a new map that becomes a part of the layout of our brain; this new map literally becomes part of who we are.

Our brains like to create order out of the chaos of data coming into them, to make links between information so that our lives make more sense. We feel more comfortable surrounded by order, we feel better inside symmetry, where we can see how everything is connected. Thus we are constantly making links between maps to form new metamaps. A field called *Gestalt psychology*[3] has done significant research on how we look at situations and make meaning out of them.

One respected theory for why our brain likes to make everything fit together is that our maps help us predict the outcome of situations more easily. In *On Intelligence,*[4] Jeff Hawkins, founder of Palm Computing, puts forward that our predictive abilities are the attributes that differentiate us most from the rest of the animal kingdom. The first time we use a new computer we're confused as to where the shortcut buttons are: after a few days we have a mental map for how to hit them, and could do so with our eyes closed. The more hardwired our maps are for repetitive tasks, the more we've freed up our working memory for higher-level tasks.

Let's get back to what happens when we create new mental maps. You can tell when you are going through this process yourself because you will probably stop speaking and start picturing concepts in your own mind. You can tell when other people are going through this process: their eyes become glazed, they reflect, and they often look up or away into the distance. When we are processing complex ideas we tap into our visual center: we see ideas as flashes in our mind's eye.

We've all had the feeling of that sudden "aha" moment. It's a moment when various ideas that were not linked before come together to form a new idea. It feels like we've seen something new. This is the moment of creation of a new map. There is a big release of energy when this new map forms, even though energy was required up front to connect the dots. There's a tale told about Archimedes, who after an insight about how to solve a scientific challenge, leaped out of the bath and ran through the streets naked shouting "Eureka!"[5] Such is the impact that insights can have on us.

When we create a new map we feel motivated to do something, and our face and voice change. When you watch for it, you can see that the act of creating a new map is a specific event. It's possible to pinpoint the exact moment it occurs. This is the moment of breakthrough, a moment when we see an answer to a challenge or problem. We'll explore the anatomy of these aha moments further in the chapter called Dance Toward Insight, where we'll go into exactly what happens in the brain during the few seconds before, while, and after we generate a new idea.

Consider what happens when we want to think a new thought, process a set of ideas, make a decision, or unravel any kind of issue. For example, as a manager you might want to increase the sales in your division but are not sure you have the right people on board. Or as an executive you need to decide whether or not to confront a manager about their poor performance. In each instance we need to create a new map in our brain. We literally have to "think things through for ourselves." It is important to realize this is still the case even when we are told what we "should" do; unless that "should" fits exactly with our existing wiring (which as you will see in the next insight is extremely unlikely), we still need to expend the energy to create our own maps.

Creating a new map chews up resources. Our brain needs to do a lot of comparing, associating, and matching any new idea with our existing maps. However, the creation of the new map releases substantial energy along with various neurotransmitters, and even changes the brain waves occurring. There is a sudden, strong motivation for action.

So let's stop for a moment and reflect on the ideas I have put forward so far, and see what they might add up to.

1. To take any kind of committed action, people need to think things through for themselves;
2. People experience a degree of inertia around thinking for themselves due to the energy required;
3. The act of having an aha moment gives off the kind of energy needed for people to become motivated and willing to take action

It becomes clear why our job as leaders should be to help people make their own connections. Instead of this, much of our energy goes into trying to do the thinking *for* people, and then seeing if our ideas stick. As you will see in the next insight, this is usually a big waste of human resources. (And I mean that in every sense of the word.)

There is a new world to explore here. If we are trying to help other people think, we might develop a whole new set of skills—such as the ability to create the physical and mental space for people to want to think, the ability to help others simplify their thinking, the ability to notice certain qualities in people's thinking, the ability to help others make their own connections. These are some of the most important skills that leaders must master today, and central to being a Quiet Leader.

UP CLOSE, NO TWO BRAINS ARE ALIKE

There are more possible ways to connect the brain's neurons than there are atoms in the universe.

JOHN RATEY (2001)

As scientists have begun to understand the mechanics of the brain they have discovered a world of almost unimaginable complexity.[6] The brain has around 100 billion neurons. Each neuron may have up to 100,000 dendrites (think of dendrites as roots—they gather information for the neuron) and one axon (think of the axon as a tree trunk, passing on information). The connections between our neurons, connected by the dendrites, are the maps that guide our thoughts, behaviors, and action.

If you want to determine how many possible ways the neurons in a brain could be connected, simply multiply the number of neurons by their roots and branches, and then by the number of chemical messengers they can use to communicate. As it turns out, this is a rather ridiculous number. Let's keep it simple and just say that it's a larger number than there are atoms in the known universe, as Dr. Ratey says.[7] Some people think this means we have unlimited mind power; however, that's somewhat of a misunderstanding. Yes, the brain has extraordinary capacity to develop connections: just listen to a jazz musician in full flight to see what a well-trained brain can do.

Here is a more accurate insight from the fact that we each have more than 300 trillion constantly changing connections: There are unlimited different ways that brains can store information, unlimited options for how experience, learning, and information might be encoded in the brain.[8]

Have you noticed how different people look at the same situation from quite different perspectives? Perhaps you played telephone as a child; there is a similar game played in leadership development programs. Person one explains a new job description to person two. Person two then passes on the job description to person three. Person three then explains the job description back to person one, who is then baffled at how different the job has become after just a couple of handovers. People hear even the simplest things very differently. And the reason for this is that our brains are substantially more different than we acknowledge.

I mentioned earlier that our minds process complex ideas fastest when we use our visual resources. So let me tell you a story to illustrate how different our brains are. (Note that the phrase "process complex ideas" means that we're making our own mental maps and comparing them to our existing maps. By hearing my story you can "see" my point for yourself.)

A year ago, my wife, Lisa, bought two identical computers for each of us to use. Lisa and I have been together for nearly ten years and we know just about everything about each other. Yet after only one year of using our computers I can't make any sense of hers. It takes me a lot longer to do a basic task on her laptop than it does on mine. I don't know how she files information; I can't picture the way she's arranged her digital world.

Our environment literally shapes the physical nature of our brains; therefore our brains were already quite different to each other's at birth. Since then, the circuitry of our brain has been molded by every sound, thought, feelings, idea, and experience, for our whole lives. So while your brain looks similar to mine at a distance, the way we store, organize, manage, and retrieve information is as different between you and me as two laptops would be after forty years of use.

All this is quite logical; however, we are a long way from living like this is the truth. When we are trying to help a colleague think anything through, we make the unconscious assumption that the other person's brain works the same as ours. So we input their problem into our brain, see the connections our brain would make to solve this problem, and spit out the solution that would work for us. We then tell people what *we* would do and are convinced it's what *they* should do.

I have watched this happen hundreds of times in my workshops and in day-to-day life. Highly successful, intelligent people are blind to the fact that they are trying to make connections *for* people, assuming their brains are similar enough for this to work. Even those people you would consider emotionally intelligent naturally want to do the thinking for others. It is a rare person indeed who doesn't try to help another human being on the assumption that their brains are basically the same.

Doing the thinking for other people is not just a waste of our own energy; it also gets in the way of other people working out the right answers. Consider for a moment how much advice you get each week from others. Putting aside information we couldn't find for ourselves, like a password, how often is the advice people give you truly useful?

Our mental maps are so remarkably different, yet we live as if this is not the case. To me, the implications of this insight are almost as significant as seeing the Earth is actually round. If the world truly accepted this insight we might see the foundations of education, training, and development shaken up, which I'm not alone in thinking could be a positive thing. To you, of course, this insight may bring to mind implications I couldn't possibly predict.

■ ■ ■ ■ ■ ■ ■ EXERCISE STATION FOR ■ ■ ■ ■ ■ ■ ■ ■

Up Close, No Two Brains Are Alike

If you'd like to take this insight further, here is an exercise that you might like (or, of course, you might come up with a much better one). For one whole week keep a tally of the number of times people give you advice, and the number of times it is useful. At the end of the week do the math to see the percentage that advice was useful to you. See what happens in how you approach others around you after that.

_____

_____

_____

_____

_____

_____

_____

_____

THE BRAIN HARDWIRES
EVERYTHING IT CAN

*The brain is constantly trying to automate processes, thereby dispelling
them from consciousness; in this way, its work will be completed faster,
more effectively and at a lower metabolic level. Consciousness, on the
other hand, is slow, subject to error and "expensive."*

GERHARD ROTH (2004)

I discovered something about my own wiring while watching my
one-year-old daughter, Trinity, learning to walk. At that time I was
living in an apartment that was up two flights of stairs. Though they
were carpeted, the stairs were steep enough to cause harm if Trinity
toppled over. Early on during the process of learning to walk that's
exactly what she did, and the resulting scream, the intense fatherly
guilt of causing her pain, and the fear of causing long-term harm led
the incident to be firmly wired into my brain.[9] Every time I went out
with Trinity after this event I purposefully took her by the hand
down the stairs, and she hasn't fallen since. I can't be sure if there was
any change in Trinity's brain, but I know that in my brain, the wiring
was quite different from that point on. And so far, nine months later,
my brain is still different. I had learned something.

Recent findings from neuroscience are showing that when we
learn, the universe changes too. The connections between our neurons reconfigure, and the world is a tiny bit different as a result.

When I saw Trinity fall down the stairs, the impact of this experience was strong enough to create what is termed *hard wiring* in my brain. A specific thought pops up each time I take the stairs with her, and that thought is now a part of my life, a new habit that I live by. This thought is now an automatic function, and in several years' time, when Trinity is quite adept at taking the stairs, I will probably still feel the urge to take her hand.

This habit is not being held in my working memory; it's hardwired somewhere deeper. We have a limited amount of working memory, which anyone who has tried to juggle too many projects at once has discovered. Joseph LeDoux, a renowned neuroscientist working at New York University, believes that the brain can hold just seven concepts in working memory at any time.[10] Therefore the brain likes to take any action or thought that is repeated, or tagged as important in any way (which seems to be linked to the amount of emotional charge in an event), and in a sense "hard code" them. The brain pushes the map down into the part of itself that holds long-term memories and processes, called the subcortex, which has far more capacity than working memory.

An analogy for hard wiring is the way water flows across the surface of the Earth. The water finds a course through the land, and over time this course deepens and it becomes less and less likely that water will flow another way. The Grand Canyon was created like this. In the same way, we develop chemical and physical links between our neurons, which over time become more ingrained, to the point that eventually we would only be able to forge a new pathway with quite some effort. It's like treading a well-worn path through thick jungle versus having to cut a new route—the well-trodden path is so much easier.

When you learn to play a new sport, for example tennis, your skills improve quite quickly. That's because your brain hardwires some of your movements as you go along. This allows you to forget about, say, how to hold your racquet, and now focus on your stance. Brain scans of elite athletes have shown that they use significantly less of their brain while playing their sport, compared to nonelite athletes.[11] You would think intuitively it would be the other way around, but what's happening is that the bulk of the athlete's cognitive brain is no longer required for their movements, and can be used just for high-level decision making as needed. They have trained their brain as much as their body. It seems our hard wiring is more dependable, more able to deliver results, than our everyday consciousness.

So the way we talk, walk, interact, read emails, and manage our staff is, for the most part, deeply hardwired and therefore habitual. Our habits are literally unconscious to us; we don't "have in mind" what we are doing. You might take this further and say that once people have done a job for some time, they are unconscious much of their workday.

In summary, given how deeply hardwired we all are, if we want to help others change any type of habit, it's going to take more effort than we are currently applying, and possibly a whole new approach.

OUR HARD WIRING DRIVES
AUTOMATIC PERCEPTION

Prediction is not just one of the things your brain does. It is the primary function of the neocortex, and the foundation of intelligence.

JEFF HAWKINS (2004)

This next insight is a radical one, and it's one that's taken many neuroscientists by surprise. However, it's something that writers, philosophers, and poets have been pondering for a few thousand years. It wasn't hard for an ancient Greek scholar to notice that doctors always saw diseases, that children saw opportunities for mayhem, and that mathematicians saw logic in everything. In the last thirty years as the New Age movement took on the role of global philosopher, the mantra of "you create your own reality" has been repeated in seemingly infinite forms. From Napoleon Hill to Dr. Phil, from Deepak Chopra to Oprah, millions of books and workshops have churned out the message, put so eloquently by Anaïs Nin, that we see the world as *we* are, not as the world is.[12]

Let's look at how this happens in the brain. Any piece of information that comes along, whether it's a new face, a new way of thinking about ourselves, or a new business idea, gets broadly the same treatment when it enters the brain. It doesn't matter whether the data is in the form of a force, a sound, a smell, a taste, an image, or a texture,[13] the process is that the new data is compared to our existing mental maps, to see where the connections are. We then try to fit the data into our existing frameworks. If any data doesn't quite fit, we try harder to make the connections, we literally try to make the connections fit. Perhaps you have noticed that when we are for an idea we are more likely to allow tenuous links to become fact, and when we are against an idea we see even strong evidence as irrelevant. Even whole societies do that collectively at times.

While our brain likes to fit every piece of new information into an existing map, it's dealing with a massive volume of information. Millions of pieces of data pour in through our senses each second, at the same time as complex internal data processing takes place. The way we can process such massive volumes of data is by doing a lot of *approximating*. For example, once we have learned to read, we read by glancing over the first letter or two of a word and guessing the rest, in the context of the whole sentence and the word after it.

What does the phrase below, from a famous Disney movie, say to you?

> *When you wish*
> *upon a a star . . .*

We expect the sentence to say "when you wish upon a star" because we've heard this phrase before, yet most people won't see that there are two *a*'s in the sentence. We see the sentence according to our expectations, not based on what is in front of us. As a consequence, we get a lot of things wrong.

Here's a story I won't forget in a hurry about how my own brain once got things wrong. A few years ago while in another country I wanted to get a local phone chip for my cell phone, a SIM card as they're called, so that I could have a local phone number and avoid international phone bills. Lisa kindly offered to handle this for me. A few days later she handed me my phone as I headed off to a conference, saying, "It's done." Or at least that's what I thought she said; in fact, she'd said something quite different. So off I went, making many more calls than I would have otherwise. At one point I called a colleague to give him my new number. "That's weird," he said. "Your old number is showing up on my screen." "Oh, that must be just a weird type of phone memory," I responded. I can actually remember pushing aside the flicker of a thought that came through my mind with another thought, which went "Naah, that's not possible." My reality was firmly set in place, and I had defense mechanisms to ensure the world stayed the way I expected it to be.

Several days later while chatting with Lisa on my cell I thanked her for organizing the new chip. "How did you manage to get the battery off?" she asked. "What are you talking about?" I responded, my wiring starting to overload. She told me to look in the coin section of my wallet and there, to my horror, was the new chip. And boy, did I feel silly, not to mention poor when the bill came in a month later.

In the story above, my brain was seeing the world through my wiring, even when strong evidence to the contrary was showing up. It's like when you close a big deal one week and nothing seems hard. Then you discover the deal's fallen apart, and the same projects seem like wading through mud. It is our interpretations of the facts, the decisions our brains make of inputs around us, that determine how we perceive reality. There is literally no reality "out there," only the reality we are deciding to see. Our automatic perceptions are driven by our hardwiring.[14] Some of this wiring is only short term, held in our working memory such as a bad mood that passes after a day. However, some of our wiring is very long term indeed. Many of our habits are driven by decisions we made in the past that are now literally a part of us. Finding ways to shift these hardwired habits is often the central challenge for leaders as they try to bring out the best in their people.

Let's reflect on all this a little. Our brain tries to make whatever we are sensing or thinking fit into our existing mental models. It does so through guesswork that's based on past experience, which has been hardwired in our brain. If we think the world is a dangerous place, we look around for evidence of this and find it. If we think people are talking about us, we find evidence for this too. Whatever filter we hold in mind, the brain will look for evidence to confirm this filter, and it does this extremely efficiently, second to second, without our conscious mind being aware of what we are doing.

I'm not saying this is all a bad thing, in fact perceiving the world through hardwiring is very useful: Without it we couldn't cope with the volume of information hitting our senses every moment, nor could we speak, read, write, or do business. And now comes the good news: If our world is defined by the mental frames we hold in mind, it means it's possible to tangibly improve people's performance simply by helping them shift their thinking.

The link between hard wiring and perception explains many business performance trends, from visualization to the power of setting goals to the impact of positive feedback on others. As a leader who wants to improve other people's performance, it's going to be useful to be able to influence the way people perceive the world. This is a new art for most leaders, one that requires the development of new muscles.

So there are big upsides to the fact that we perceive the world according to our wiring. Now let's explore the downsides.

1. Changing the way people think is one of the tougher challenges of leadership, as people tend to fight hard to hold on to their view of the world. They feel that if they change their thinking the whole world might collapse, and in a sense this is true, given that we perceive the world through our mental maps. Confronting people head-on can make them dig their heels in further. A more subtle approach may be needed here.

2. When external realities change, people's internal realities often don't change as quickly. When experiencing a big change at work, employees literally need time to rewire their minds. And they have to make their own connections, according to their own wiring. We can make the space for this to happen, and encourage it, but then we need to take a step back and allow the process to unfold.

3. Given that our wiring is all so different, any group of people

will see the same situation from substantially different perspectives. Rather than fighting this fact, the best leaders harness this reality by bringing together a balanced team of people who think in different ways. When two people think too much alike they get in each other's way.

4. Some people's maps could be out of date. Someone may perceive others at work as a threat, as a result of difficulties in a previous job. Helping people identify and then let go of mental frames that are holding them back from performing at their peak is another important skill for leaders to develop.

The implications of the fact that our hard wiring drives perceptions are far reaching, and of course will be different for each reader. Yet although people have been discussing this idea for decades now, in the corporate world this insight is a long way from being at the forefront. The brain truly sees the world according to its own wiring. In fact, the majority of the time it's even worse than that—our brains will go to great pains to vehemently defend our existing mental models even to the point, at times, of death.[15]

IT'S PRACTICALLY IMPOSSIBLE
TO DECONSTRUCT OUR WIRING

*Connections that are used become stronger,
even permanent elements of the neural circuitry.*

Jeffrey M. Schwartz and Sharon Begley (2002)

We've explored how our habits, thoughts, aptitudes, and skills are based on unimaginably complex sets of connections that can't be accurately predicted. Many of these connections are firmly embedded into our subconscious. These connections then define how we see the world, the choices we make, and therefore the results we produce, without our knowledge that this is happening. So if we want to improve a person's performance, the obvious next question is how do we change their connections? The answer, it turns out, is that unfortunately we can't. It's almost impossible to change any hard wiring that's been embedded in the brain.

Now, I am not saying that the brain has no ability to change—clearly with a million new connections being created each second there is an awful lot of change going on. However, the *way* we go about trying to change our habits most of the time is fundamentally flawed.[16] Our default mode for trying to change our habits is to try to "unwire" what is already there, to deconstruct it somehow.[17] However, it's like trying to get rid of the Grand Canyon—it's not such an easy task. Far easier to leave it where it is, cut a small new path in the side of the wall and allow the water to do its work over time.

Let's take a deeper look at the mechanics of what happens when we try to change our wiring. Our automatic approach is to deconstruct the habit, meaning to try to understand where it comes from. We are a reductionist society: Our tendency is to assume that knowing the source of an issue will resolve it. So when we want to change something about ourselves, we first look down into our memory and search for the roots of our habits. We look for the links. We literally try to make connections from the habit back into our past; in the process we deepen the connections between the idea that we want to replace and other parts of our brain. Can you see where I am going with this?

Given how interconnected the brain is, we can probably find links just about anywhere we look. It's easy to be lured into the fascinating world of links, connections, and reasons, and continue down the rabbit hole for a long time, even our whole lives. Not confident speaking in public? Think about it hard enough and you'll find lots of reasons why. Maybe it's your confidence, which is poor because of a lack of positive feedback when you were young. Maybe it's a fear of being open. Maybe it's something that happened when you were at school. While these connections might be interesting to talk about, how useful is this process of finding the reasons and links? Will seeing these links, even if they are true, help us change the habit? Also, remember that with the brain's tendency to find what it's looking for, we may create links that were not even there in the first place.

Now, just to be clear, I am talking about what we do once we have basic awareness of a habit we want to change. I am not saying we shouldn't reflect and learn about ourselves—far from it. Becoming more conscious of the way we move through the world is a critical first step to fulfilling our potential in any domain. However, it's what we do once we've seen something we want to change that makes all the difference. Looking for the source of a habit literally creates more connections between this habit and other parts of our brain. The more we focus on a problem we have, the more ingrained we make it.

So what about just telling ourselves to "stop it"? Unfortunately, hard wiring is quite firmly implanted. What usually happens is we fail to stop the habit, and then become upset with ourselves for failing. This provides further links and energy to the original wiring we wanted to get rid of, further embedding the habit.

There is another way: We can leave the problem wiring where it is, and focus wholly and completely on the creation of new wiring. This is just what happens in the brain when we are solutions-focused. Yet for many people, the act of focusing solely on creating new wiring requires the creation of new wiring in itself.

In summary, science is showing that we *can* change the way we think, and that it's not as hard as we've been assuming. Changing a habit, now that's hard, but leaving it where it is and creating a whole new habit—that turns out to be far more achievable. There are many implications to all this, and this insight and the next one combined are ideas we draw on heavily for the rest of this book. To start with, in a workplace context this insight means that if you're trying to improve people's performance, then working out what's wrong with their thinking is not going to be very productive. Again, we need a whole new approach.

IT'S EASY TO CREATE NEW WIRING

*Whenever you read a book or have a conversation,
the experience causes physical changes in your brain.*

GEORGE JOHNSON (1991)

Until just twenty years ago scientists thought our brain was all wired up by early childhood, and then slowly declined in complexity, with neurons dying away over time and our links becoming weaker as we aged. The theory was that we couldn't regrow or make new connections between our neurons. This seemed logical given that children went through a phase of easy learning which slowed down at a certain point, and that we seemed to become more forgetful as we got older. All this has changed with an exciting new domain within neuroscience called neuroplasticity.

Neuroplasticity grew out of studies of stroke patients and those with other degenerative brain diseases.[18] Scientists found that the brain had a remarkable ability to rewire itself when things went wrong. If the part of the brain responsible for speech was affected by disease, other parts of the brain could be called into action and would start to perform this function. The brain diverted traffic along new highways it quickly laid down around the accident site, allowing largely normal functioning to occur.

As the study of the plasticity of the brain evolved, scientists noticed that the brain was capable of creating new connections on a massive scale, at any stage of life, and did this in response to anything new that was learned, such as learning to play an instrument. Edward Taub initiated much of the breakthrough work in this realm in the 1980s, at the time as the chief scientist at the Institute for Behavioral Research in Silver Spring, Maryland. As did Michael Merzenich of the University of California in San Francisco.[19] However, for years mainstream neuroscience strongly resisted Taub's and Merzenich's results. Finally, by the mid- and particularly late 1990s, through advances in imaging technology together with results reported from stroke patients, it became widely accepted that the brain could rewire itself as a result of physical therapy.[20]

It is now widely believed that our brain doesn't just get rewired when life-changing events occur; it happens second by second, day and night, in response to everything going on around us. Every day we create enormous sets of new maps that change the chemical and physical connections in our brain. Drive to a suburb you've never visited before and you will feel a sense of not being able to picture where you're going and feel mild anxiety. By visiting the area just once, even for a few minutes, you automatically create a mental map of the suburb. Go back five years later and you will, quite literally, still have that map in mind: as a result you feel less anxious than if you'd never been there before. Your brain's wiring was changed by your visit.

Everything we think and do influences the layout and connections of our brain. Every thought, word, new idea, what we eat, what we do for exercise, how we define ourselves—all of this and more is fine-tuning the pathways inside our head. The upside to this finding is that we have an incredible ability to change, an immense capacity for new connections. Our brain is very comfortable making new maps, perhaps you could even say it's the brain's favorite activity.

You have created hundreds of millions of new connections from reading this book so far. However, most of these won't be hardwired into long-term memory. Right now you can probably remember the major points you've read, but if you didn't do anything else with these ideas it's unlikely you'd remember this book in detail in two years' time. So there is clearly a difference between a thought (a map held in our working memory), and a habit (a map that's hardwired in the deeper parts of our brain).

Science is showing it's not that difficult to bridge the gap between a thought and a habit. If we want to hardwire a new behavior we just need to give our new mental map enough attention, over enough time, to ensure it becomes embedded in our brain. We do this by making links to different parts of the brain so that the web of links thickens and spreads out. Instead of just thinking about an idea, we also write it down, and speak about it, and take action. These events provide links across many parts of the brain, such that our new map has more depth, more density, and is thus held in place more firmly. If we literally put enough energy into the insight or idea, it will become a part of who we are. It's an attention economy in our brains, at a million connections per second.

Lots of research has been done on this fascinating gap—the gap between a thought and a habit—by fields as diverse as neuroscience, sports psychology, education, adult learning theory, behavioral science, and cognitive behavioral therapy. Here are some of the findings that are most relevant here.

1. *New habits take time, but not that much:* For a long time it's been commonly believed that it takes several months before we create a new habit—in other words, hardwire a new behavior into our thinking. However, science is showing that we create both chemical and physical changes in our brain remarkably quickly. Studies show[21] that physical new branches, called dendrites, were emerging after just an hour of stimulation. Try opening your car door with your other hand for one day and watch what happens. It doesn't take long to create new habits. What's hard is trying to *uncreate* them.

2. *Positive feedback is essential:* This quote from *What Makes You Tick* by Thomas Czerner says it so well: "The brain needs to see a happy face and to hear occasional laughter to cement its neural circuitry. The encouraging sounds of 'Yes! Good! That's it!' help to mark a synapse for preservation rather than pruning."

We'll go further into the importance of positive feedback at several other points later in the book. Suffice to say for now that neurons literally need positive feedback in some form to create long-term connections.[22] If we want to help people improve their performance at work, we need to become much more proficient at giving positive feedback.

3. *Too many thoughts, too little time:* One of the difficulties inherent in developing new wiring is simply *remembering* to do what we know we *should* do. We need to remember to remember, something that's quite a challenge in a week overloaded with priorities and deadlines. This is why it can make such a difference having another person help us change. The reminder, the attention, the energy of knowing someone is thinking about our new habit, helps create more links to the insight we are attempting to hold in mind. Put another way, we can make a tremendous difference to other people's thinking by helping them clearly identify the insights they would like to hardwire, and over time reminding them about these insights.[23]

You might be wondering what happens to our old wiring when we create new maps. Wouldn't there be a conflict between the old and new? A new field of neuroscience called neural Darwinism[24] is studying how the brain constantly prunes and removes unused links. Just as your ability to do complex mathematical multiplications in your head quickly in your youth largely disappears if not used for years, any pathways you don't use for a while slowly become less connected. So if you want to change your habits, just give less energy to the habits you don't like. Like pesky neighbors whom you'd rather not deal with, don't bother them and they won't bother you. Meanwhile clearly define the new connections you'd like to foster and get to work at turning these into long-term habits.

In summary, if we want to improve people's performance, our job is to help them find new ways to approach situations that leaves their existing wiring where it is, and allows for the development and ultimately the hard wiring of new habits. A less technical way of saying this is we need to help people focus on solutions instead of problems. We need to give up our desire to find behaviors to fix, and become fascinated with identifying and growing people's strengths, an entirely other discipline.

SUMMARIZING THE RECENT DISCOVERIES ABOUT THE BRAIN

The brain was constructed to change.

MICHAEL MERZENICH (1992)

Our standard practices for improving performance involve techniques that are largely ineffective at helping others: giving advice, solving problems, or trying to work out how people need to think. To maximize our effectiveness as leaders, it's time to give up second guessing what peoples' brains need, and become masters of helping others think for themselves. The best way to do that is by defining solutions rather than problems, and helping people identify for themselves new habits they could develop to bring those solutions closer. Pivotal to all this is the art of enabling other people to have their own insights.

Once people have had new insights for themselves, our job as quiet leaders is to provide the encouragement, ongoing support and belief in people, over time, to ensure they develop the new habits that are possible. Then we will be truly bringing out the best in others. As it turns out, this new approach saves a tremendous amount of time and energy for everyone involved.

If you're still wondering exactly how you're going to do all this, you're in just the right place as that's precisely what the rest of this book is about.

■ ■ ■ ■ ■ ■ ■ EXERCISE STATION FOR ■ ■ ■ ■ ■ ■ ■ ■

All the Recent Discoveries About the Brain that Change Everything

If you've had some useful insights from reading this book so far, now could be a great time to deepen them by writing your ideas down. The act of taking time to crystallize high-level thoughts, images, and connections into concrete words, and then writing them down is, as you know by now, one of the ways to cajole our delicate new wiring into hard wiring: to ensure an insight becomes not just a good idea but a part of who we are.

_____

_____

_____

_____

_____

_____

_____

Part Two

The Six Steps to Transforming Performance

We may need to solve problems not by removing the cause but by designing the way forward even if the cause remains in place.

EDWARD DE BONO

ABOUT THE SIX STEPS

The insights we've explored about the brain point to a new way of improving other people's performance, and a platform on which to build the rest of the book. However, I doubt that just knowing these insights is going to turn anyone into a Quiet Leader overnight. We need more explicit, practical, and visible signposts to help us follow this new path. That's what the Six Steps to Transforming Performance provide.

The Six Steps evolved over years of running performance coaching workshops for thousands of people. By doing the same types of exercises over and over with so many different people, I was able to see lots of fascinating patterns in how people tried to coach each other. One pattern I saw early on was that conversations had a limited number of possible directions to go in, which I have illustrated below in figure 2 below. A conversation could go north and get too philosophical, or south and get too detailed. It could go west and focus on the problem or east and focus on solutions.

There was one general direction that always seemed faster than all the others. This was to focus firmly on solutions, without getting into the details. Once I had identified which direction was the fastest to focus on in any conversation, my next goal was to identify the path of least resistance, the shortest

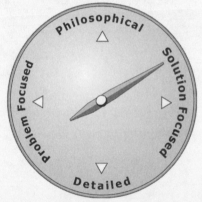

Figure 2, Directions Conversations Can Go

path from A to B: where point A was our desire to have a positive impact on another person, and point B was having a useful impact on them. I have illustrated this in figure 3 on the following page.

Over time and through watching hundreds of people try out different ideas, I gradually began to identify a process map for these most efficient conversations. This process map had many different parts to it that all tied together, and the map itself was independent of the content of any dialogue. Over several years I built and tested many different ways of communicating this map to others, keeping what worked and refining what didn't. Eventually this work formed into the set of ideas I now call the

Six Steps to Transforming Performance, as well as some other tools I may introduce in a later book.

Figure 3, The Shortest Route from A to B

The Six Steps describe a new way for leaders to have conversations when they truly want to make a difference in another person's performance. These steps describe a new way to interact, a new way to give feedback, a new way to influence, a new way to stretch and grow people, a new way to bring out the best in others.

The great news is that this new way *saves time* and *creates energy*. My experience is that I can often get from A to B in just five minutes using the Six Steps: When I don't remember to follow the steps, I am sometimes still going in circles after an hour. The Six Steps describe the path of least resistance when you want to help someone learn or change.

Now that I've given you an idea of how the Six Steps were developed, let's explore how the Six Steps relate to brain functioning. When a person is struggling to perform at their best at anything, it means they have not yet been able to "think their way out of a situation." There is something they want to achieve, yet there is a "but" in the way; they have a dilemma or mental impasse. For example, a sales rep wants to hit his targets but has no time left for phone calls after emails. He needs to create new mental maps to process his world more efficiently. The Six Steps are a structured way of helping people do just that.

The drawing, on page 32, is a visual representation of the Six Steps. This diagram may not make much sense just yet, but as we go through each step you may find this diagram helpful to come back to.

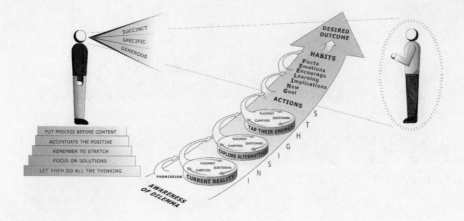

Figure 4, The Six Steps to Transforming Performance

The first step to transforming performance is learning to Think About Thinking. This is the platform that the leader, the person on the left in this picture, is standing on. Much of the first step links directly with the recent insights about the brain; we explore the concept of staying out of the details and letting the other person do the heavy thinking; we look at the importance of staying solutions-focused; and what positive feedback does for thinking. We look into the ideas of stretching people's thinking and the concept of having good process in any dialogue.

The second step, Listen for Potential, is about listening for where people are heading, rather than for what might not be working. In the diagram above you can see the leader listening to the whole person, in a sense. In order to do this we need to maintain what I call The Clarity of Distance: a clear frame of mind, seeing people as their potential, not through our own filters or agendas.

Step three is called Speak with Intent. Here we work on improving the quality of every word we use when we are trying to improve others' thinking. In the diagram above you can see this step as defining the quality of every word that comes out of the leader's mouth.

The fourth step is called Dance Toward Insight, where we look at the first layer of the process map for dialogues that improve people's thinking. The Dance Toward Insight is a central model that helps keep you on the right conversational path, that shortest distance from A to B. In the diagram above, the Dance Toward Insight model consists of the elements of permission, placement, questioning, and clarifying, that sit inside the disks between the leader and their employee.

Step five is called CREATE New Thinking, and it's built around a thinking tool called the CREATE model. The CREATE model shows you the higher-level patterns that occur when you Dance Toward Insight, to help you have the most efficient conversation possible. CREATE is made up of the three disks in the diagram, Current Reality, Explore Alternatives, and Tap Their Energy.

The final step is called Follow Up. This step is about making sure people's new thinking becomes reality, closing the gap between an idea and a habit. Here we explore the FEELING model, something that reminds us of what to pay attention to when we follow up. You can see in the diagram that the FEELING models sits directly between an action someone has taken, and a habit that is formed.

Although I am explaining the Six Steps in a linear fashion, using them in conversations is not a linear process. Each step does need to be mastered before you can achieve the best outcome of the following step; however, when you use the model it's not a follow-the-bouncing-ball-type conversation. It's more like learning to play the piano. You need to learn how to read music and hold your hands, and integrate the concept of rhythm, but you don't play by doing those three things one after the other—it all happens together when you play. As with anything that you learn in stages, the early steps may make more sense when you see how they fit with the later steps. It's like building a house: While each element is interesting on its own, it's when all the steps come together that you have something useful to live in. Also many people who read the book before publication told me the Six Steps fell into place in their mind when they saw the models being used in real situations, which happens in the third section of the book, called Putting the Six Steps to Use.

In summary, the Six Steps are signposts that point to a new path to follow whenever we enter a conversation with the intent of helping another person change in any way. Whether we want others to sell more, manage better, or be more thorough, motivated, organized, focused, or self-aware, the Six Steps show us a new way to improve performance without telling anyone what to do. This new way—the way of the Quiet Leader—saves time, creates energy, and transforms performance.

THINK ABOUT THINKING

One cannot teach a man anything.
One can only enable him to learn from within himself.

GALILEO GALILEI (1564–1642)

Figure 5, Think About Thinking

The first step to being a Quiet Leader is to think about people's thinking. In other words, to become passionate about improving not *what* people are thinking about, but the *way* they think.

There are five elements to this step. The first element is to let the other person think through their own issue, rather than telling them what to do. This is the underlying and most important principle in the whole book: without this approach, nothing that comes after it will help. Once you've got people doing the thinking, you need to keep them focused on solutions, so that conversations are as useful as possible. Next, if you want to bring out people's best you need to stretch and challenge them, to open up their thinking, not just be supportive. At the same time as stretching, you also need to focus on the positive, on what people are doing well, so that you grow people's strengths. And finally, you need to do everything you can to make it easy for people to think, by having a clear process behind every conversation. Let's take a look at each of these elements now.

LET THEM DO ALL THE THINKING

Ideas are like children, there are none so wonderful as your own

CHINESE FORTUNE COOKIE (2005)

Figure 6, Let Them Do All the Thinking

Most large organizations are now set up to hire only the best and the brightest, people who've already proven themselves to be highly successful individuals. Right here is one of the challenges: the more successful an individual is, the less you can tell them what to do, and the more you can only help them think better for themselves.

Let's explore this idea in a dialogue between two people. Sally is a bank manager in charge of a large branch, responsible for around thirty staff members. She's having a conversation with one of her employees, Paul, who is responsible for the sales team. Paul has just said to Sally, "I really don't know how to lift our sales right now." Sally does what most managers might do, and says, "It's important to get our sales moving so we hit our targets. I think you need to get more focused and put more time into this, the deadline is coming up fast."

This mini dialogue is similar to the millions of interactions that occur every day in the workplace. Sally is trying to help Paul perform better, but she's using a blunt instrument: telling Paul what to do. As a result, Paul is unlikely to be motivated or inspired by the interaction. Her *impact* turns out to be different than her *intent*, as is so often the case with interactions of this kind.

So what would another approach look like, where Paul was doing more of the thinking? There's no one specific set of words that are just right; the main issue is that Paul is the one directing the conversation. So in this case Sally might ask questions like: "How can I best help you think this through?" Then she might ask questions like:

"When you say you're not sure about the project, which part of this do you want to discuss with me?"

"How much has this been on your mind?"

"Do you know what to do next and just need a sounding board, or are you really stuck?"

"How can I best help you with your thinking?"

These types of questions will get Paul starting to think, as we will explore later.

Suddenly Sally's not doing the thinking about the sales, she's thinking about how to get Paul thinking. The technical term for this is that Sally has *facilitated a self-directed learning process*.

How would you feel if you were Paul this time?

I have created a continuum below to illustrate the difference between Sally's two approaches. The right-hand side of the scale represents conversations in which Sally positively impacts Paul. The left side represents conversations in which Sally has a negative impact on him. My guess is Sally's first response would be about a negative five: It would annoy Paul somehow. Sally's second response would have most likely helped Paul, had a positive impact of, say, plus five. The difference between the negative five and plus five is ten points. A very big difference.

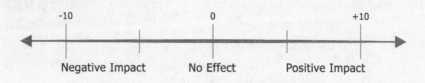

Figure 7, Positive to Negative Continuum

Here's an easy way to picture the idea of self-directed learning. Imagine you're talking to someone whose performance you'd like to improve.

The issue you're working on might be how to deal with a deadline. Let's conceptually put that issue on the table. Imagine that what you're talking about is sitting in front of both people as a physical object. Now, if you're facilitating self-directed learning, as the leader you're not interested in the issue on the table, you're interested in the other person's thinking processes. The person opposite, on the other hand, would be thinking about the issue on the table. You can see this illustrated on page 39, Figure 8.

In the second case of Sally and Paul, Sally has stood back and allowed Paul to do the thinking; she's focusing her energy on helping him think.

There are five big reasons why a self-directed approach is so useful when we are trying to improve performance: People still need to make their own connections about anything you tell them; you'll never guess the right answer anyway; it allows people to be energized

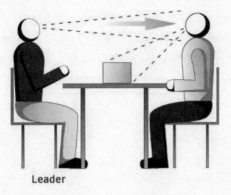

Leader

Figure 8, Focus on Their Thinking, Not the Issue on the Table

by new connections; it's less effort; and it's faster. Let's explore these reasons a bit further.

As we saw in Part One regarding the brain, being self-directed is the only way we learn, think, invent, create, solve problems, visualize, rethink, re-engineer—you name it, it all happens within a process of making our own connections. It comes down to whether we improve people's thinking or we get in the way of their thinking. If we want people to think better, let them do all the thinking, then help them think.

Many of us believe we can think for people, yet when it comes to the way we process information, our brains are all dramatically different. What we think another person should be doing is just what *our* brain might want to do, which is very unlikely to be the right idea for them. So if we want to improve the quality of their thinking, our best option is to help them process ideas better: things like helping people make their ideas more clear, or find relationships between concepts, or prioritize their thoughts.

When people make deep, new connections in their own mind, there is a tangible release of energy, a discernable "aha" moment that fills us with a desire to take action. On a physical level, this aha moment releases chemicals in the body to prime it for movement. The energy created by insight is an important energy source to be harnessed. In the workplace there are many drains on our energy, including restrictions, policies, politics, long hours, and hundreds of emails every day. We should be harnessing every possible energy source that might inspire better performance. Letting people come up with their own ideas is a deep well of motivation to tap.

When we try to think for people it takes a lot of mental energy on our part. We think hard, and still come up with the wrong answers for that person. They then fend off our ideas instead of generating their own thoughts, then we start again and try another angle. All told, there's a lot of wasted energy on both sides.

Some leaders think it's their job to tell people what to do or have all the answers. However, from watching hundreds of managers learn a few basic techniques, it's black and white to me that it takes a fraction of the time to get a positive outcome to any kind of problem using a self-directed approach than it does making suggestions. My anecdotal research shows that it takes just 10 percent to 20 percent of the time.

Managers often complain about how they have to constantly solve their people's problems—sometimes I sense it is the manager more addicted to this than the staff. Giving people an answer does little but continue their dependence on you. Anytime a person wants your help, unless it's just a password they're after, they could benefit from coming up with the answer themselves. When people use statements like: "What do you think I should . . ."; "I'm not sure what to . . ."; "I really want to . . . but I'm not . . ."; these are statements that people want help with their thinking. When you start to listen for these phrases you might notice these dialogues are happening constantly between management and their staff, and between peers, right across your organization.

Of course I am not suggesting you use this approach in every conversation; sometimes you won't have permission to have this kind of dialogue with people. Someone could just be venting at you, and the last thing they want is to think more deeply at that moment.

Here's a marker that points to situations when a self-directed approach is going to be useful: any time you feel yourself about to give

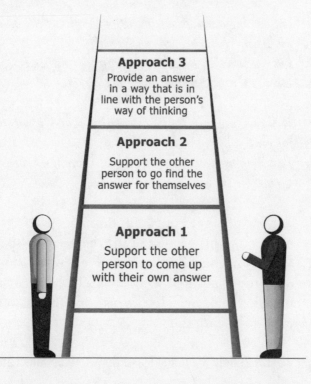

Figure 9, A Ladder of Approaches to Self-Directed Learning

advice, or about to tell a person what you would do, or wanting to share your experience or opinion. If it seems appropriate to do this, it's generally going to be appropriate to use a self-directed approach.

There are instances when a pure self-directed approach is not going to work. There is a ladder of approaches here, from 100 percent self-directed, through to partially self-directed. Always start at the pure self-directed level first before resorting to telling anyone what to do in any form.

APPROACH 1: Help Someone Make New Connections on the Spot

The first priority is always to help people come up with their own answer by making new connections themselves. In Paul and Sally's example, it might go like this:

> Paul: *I'm having a real problem with our sales at the moment.*
> Sally: *How can I best help you with this?*
> Paul: *I'm not sure . . . I just feel incredibly stretched by the budgets.*
> Sally: *Do you want to think this issue through with me right now?*
> Paul: *Sure.*
> Sally: *What's going to be the best way to do that—what would work for you?*
> Paul: *I'd like to use you as a sounding board and see what happens.*
> Sally: *Great.*

As the conversation goes on, Paul, through speaking out loud, makes a connection in his own mind that he needs to speak with a colleague about the firmness of a deadline. He realized he wasn't sure if the date was firm or not, and without this knowledge he couldn't get clear about what to do next. In this instance, the answer to Paul's dilemma lay inside his own thinking.

APPROACH 2: Help Someone Make New Connections Later

Sometimes people can't find an answer to their dilemma on the spot. In this instance, help them work out how to find the answer themselves later on, rather than just give them your answer. If you tried a self-directed approach and Paul said:

> Paul: *I'm not sure how to move ahead with this.*

In this case you might say, "So what would you need to do? For example, who would you need to talk to, so that you knew what to do next?" In this instance you are empowering people to come up with their own answers.

APPROACH 3: If Neither of These Approaches Is Possible, Provide an Answer in a Way That's Most Useful to the Person's Thinking

Sometimes you have specific information the other person needs, such as a piece of data or inside knowledge of a system. If you're not 100 percent sure you have the right answer, you might pose your idea as just a possibility. If you are clear you have specific information someone needs, you can still use a self-directed approach, by seeing how someone wants the information presented. It might go like this:

> Paul: *I'm not sure what to do about our sales situation.*
>
> Sally: *I think I may have a bit of information that might help you here. Do you want me to tell you what I think?*
>
> Paul: *Sure, great.*
>
> Sally: *Do you want the short answer or a bit of background here?*
>
> Paul: *I'd like all of the background, I think. This is a big issue right now for me. I want as much clarity as I can get.*
>
> Sally: *How much time do you want me to spend on this?*

In this third example, Sally is checking if it's okay to give Paul an answer. She's also using language that lets Paul know she's not attached to the answer. You can see this in words like "I *may* have . . . which *might possibly* help you here." This sends a signal that she respects Paul's thoughts. Then she's letting Paul decide how he wants the information. All of this puts Paul more in control, which means he's more likely to adopt any good ideas.

The self-directed approach is a way of thinking, not just a technique. It's a commitment to helping the other person do as much of the thinking as possible, according to the way their wiring is set up. It's about putting the other person's brain in the driver's seat. Of course, there are times when a directive style is more appropriate as a leader. Firing people and life-or-death emergencies need a different approach. However, in general day-to-day work, if you want to improve people's performance, make it your job to help them think better, rather than think for them. Sounds simple enough, yet this is a long way from the approach that happens in most workplaces.

In summary, Quiet Leaders know that a key part of transforming performance is getting the other person to find their own answers. This quote from Sir John Whitmore sums it up nicely: "To tell denies or negates another's intelligence. To ask honors it."

 EXERCISE STATION FOR ■ ■ ■ ■ ■ ■ ■ ■

Let Them Do All the Thinking

This week, make a note of the number of times that people try to tell you what to do or how to think. Start to notice the impact that this has on your thinking—do you appreciate when people do this? What do you do in response?

_____

_____

_____

_____

_____

_____

_____

_____

FOCUS ON SOLUTIONS

What we pay attention to, and how we pay attention,
determines the content and quality of life.

MIHALY CSIKSZENTMIHALYI (2003)

PUT PROCESS BEFORE CONTENT
ACCENTUATE THE POSITIVE
REMEMBER TO STRETCH
FOCUS ON SOLUTIONS
LET THEM DO ALL THE THINKING

Figure 10, Focus on Solutions

It might sound obvious that to improve people's performance we need to focus their thinking on solutions, rather than problems. Yet it's surprising how little we do this in practice. I've watched hundreds of people learning to interact with others using the principle of self-directed learning and somehow people always prefer to go straight to the problems.

There's nothing inherently wrong with focusing on problems: in fact, the resulting conversations are often quite interesting. The issue is that there is simply a more useful place to put our attention, which is onto solutions. *Interesting versus useful* is one of several two-part distinctions I will introduce throughout this book.

Focusing on problems leads us to the past. It leads us to try to change what can't be changed. Focusing on problems leads to blame, excuses, and justifications. It's complicated, slow, and often drains our mental energy. Focusing on solutions, however, immediately creates energy in our minds. We open up ideas and possibilities. If we want people to come up with great ideas, to think well, to reach their potential as employees, we want them focused on solutions most of the time. This doesn't mean we don't address problems—far from it; it means we address them by analyzing the way forward, instead of their causes. Let me illustrate this with the following examples:

PROBLEM FOCUS		SOLUTIONS FOCUS
Why didn't you hit your targets?	vs.	What do you need to do next time to hit your targets?
Why did this happen?	vs.	What do you want to achieve here?
Where did it all start to go wrong?	vs.	What do you need to do to move this forward?
Why do you think you're not good at this?	vs.	How can you develop strength in this area?
What's wrong with your team?	vs.	What does your team need to do to win?
Why did you do that?	vs.	What do you want to do next?
Who is responsible for this?	vs.	Who can achieve this?
Why isn't this working?	vs.	What do we need to do to make this work?

You might notice the word "why" in many of the problem-focused questions, yet there's no use of that word around solutions. Being conscious of removing the word "why" from our conversations can be a great way to remember to focus on solutions.

Looking at the examples above, even though there's only a slight difference in the wording of the questions, when you take a solutions focus, you end up having very different conversations than when you focus on the problem. Let's explore the science behind this.

We learned in Part One on the brain that our hard wiring drives automatic perception. Well, our *nonautomatic* perception is driven by how we consciously choose to focus our thinking.[1] In other words, we have the ability to consciously choose the mental filter we see through in any moment, and this choice of filters significantly affects how the world appears to us. The technical term for this is the "frame" we see through, and when we change our frame we're "reframing."

We all reframe regularly, without this skill we might not survive the emotional highs and lows of life. A few years ago, I was surfing at the start of summer, looking forward to months in the water, when I fractured my toe jumping off the rocks. Instead of being glum about not surfing all summer, I decided this would be an opportunity to write a book I'd had on hold for a while. My first book, *Personal Best*, was finished two months later.

My point here is that focusing on solutions is a choice we make in the moment. The only difference between asking "Why did this happen?" and "What shall we do about this?" is which question we choose to ask. It's a discipline, a mental habit we either already have, or can develop.

When it comes to trying to change internal habits, focusing on solutions turns out to be even more important. We discovered that it's virtually impossible to change our wiring, in the sense that the act of trying to change who we are by "getting to the bottom of our thinking" embeds that part of ourselves even deeper into our brain; whatever we pay attention to gets embedded.[2] We also know that to improve ourselves we have to create new wiring. This means if we think our problems reside inside ourselves, there is little point trying to solve them. Instead, we need to decide on the new habits we'd like to develop, and build a realistic plan to make these habits a part of our lives.

Some people take issue with the concept of only focusing on solutions, especially when it comes to trying to develop their people. They think this is just being upbeat, or overly optimistic, to the point even of being irresponsible. People with MBAs, engineering, or accounting degrees are often (though not always!) logical and analytical thinkers who enjoy delving down into problems. When analyzing and trying to change *processes,* an analytical and problem-focused approach is very useful. But when trying to change *people,* something else is needed.

Much of psychology is also focused on the problems people have. As the renowned psychologist Martin Seligman said, "Modern psychology has been co-opted by the disease model. We've become too preoccupied with repairing damage when our focus should be on building strength and resilience, especially in children."[3] There is a central assumption inside the practices of social work, family therapies, and even psychiatry, that with enough knowledge people will change.

Don't get me wrong: I am not putting down the mental health fields. Psychiatrists, psychologists, counselors, and therapists play a crucial role in society. But when you are dealing with high performing individuals in the workplace, focusing on their problems and trying to decrease them is not the best approach.

Some people also worry about what happens to our problems when we're only focusing on solutions—won't they just fester? Research from the field of solutions-focused therapy is showing that focusing on solutions is a fast and effective way of addressing quite real problems. Take a look at this quote from *The Solutions Focus:* "It is often easier to start something new than to stop something. Anything that is a habit is by definition difficult to stop. And, if change is encouraged by positive reinforcement, it is much easier to be aware of when you are taking the reinforceable action than to know when you are not doing whatever it is that you want to give up."[4]

Problems disappear into the background as solutions develop. This makes sense when you go back to the principle that our wiring drives our perceptions: the more we focus on the solutions, the more we see these solutions becoming real. We develop an upward spiral. As Jeffrey Schwartz says in *The Mind & the Brain:* "Modern neuroscience is now demonstrating what James suspected more than a century ago: that attention is a mental state (with physically describable brain state correlates) that allows us, moment by moment, to choose and sculpt how our ever-changing minds will work, [to] choose who we will be the next moment in a very real sense . . . Those choices are left embossed in physical form on our material selves."[5] In other words, focusing on solutions is a first step to creating new wiring, to changing our very nature.

If you're worried that this just sounds too easy, consider that being solutions-focused means taking responsibility for outcomes and taking action. It doesn't mean being lazy with the facts; in fact, it requires significant discipline and focus.

In summary, Quiet Leaders know that problems are interesting to discuss, but that focusing on solutions is more useful. And they have developed the discipline of catching themselves when they get problem-focused and refocusing their energy on the way ahead.

■ ■ ■ ■ ■ ■ ■ **EXERCISE STATION FOR** ■ ■ ■ ■ ■ ■ ■ ■

Focus on Solutions

The idea of this exercise is to notice what your default modes are around problem versus solutions focus. Whenever you go into a conversation with someone, notice the number of times you focus on problems versus the number of times you choose to focus on solutions. Keep a tally of this ratio, and see what happens. An example of when you are focusing on problems is when you ask a question with the word "why" in it. Summarize your thoughts below at the end of the week.

_____

_____

_____

_____

_____

_____

REMEMBER TO STRETCH

We would rather be ruined than changed,
We would rather die in our dread
Than climb the cross of the moment
And let our illusions die.

W. H. AUDEN (1907–1973)

Figure 11, Remember to Stretch

So far we've introduced two important elements of how Quiet Leaders think about thinking: they get people doing all the thinking, and put all their attention onto solutions. Figure 12 is a simple visual that describes this concept. Quiet Leaders stay in the top right quadrant.

The fastest way to transform performance, particularly with intelligent, high-functioning people, is to ask about solutions. It sounds so simple when said like that, yet it's a surprisingly rare event in the workplace.

As well as the first two principles, Quiet Leaders know that transforming performance means stretching people. They recognize that their job involves taking people to the edge of their comfort zone, so

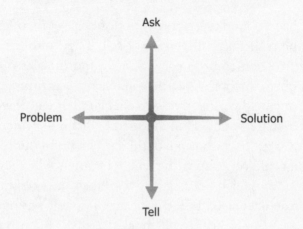

Figure 12, Ask–Tell Quadrants

they've had to learn to be comfortable with making people uncomfortable.

Change is a stretch, in both senses of the word. Bringing about change isn't easy, and it requires stretching people. Let's explore both of these concepts.

The challenge of changing behavior

A *Fast Company* magazine story in 2005 captured how hard it is to change behavior. In a study of heart attack patients, people whose lives literally depended on their ability to change habits, only one in nine of them was able to change their lifestyle.[6]

To understand why we are poor at changing our own and other people's habits, let's go back to our new understanding of the brain. We discovered that what we learn becomes hardwired, and our hard wiring drives perception. So when we try to change, we are battling against deeply embedded habits, that are not just habits to people— they are "who they are," they are reality to them. An account manager who's not confident asking for a sale from clients may have told themselves more than ten thousand times over twenty years that they are "no good at selling." This person could be the same age and socioeconomic background as a top sales performer. Yet their brain is now wired in the reality that they cannot sell. They automatically have this thought when confronted with any kind of sales opportunity. Changing them into a top salesperson means confronting the reality of their firmly held wiring, trying to change their whole world.

We learned that our default mode when helping people change is attempting to get to the bottom of their problem. In this instance the salesperson could come up with plenty of reasons why they can't sell. Yet knowing these will not help them sell better. If we want to help this person sell, we need to focus on creating new wiring. So far so good, yet even this can be a real stretch.

To simplify a little, the brain has two different qualities of internal machinery: the conscious mind ("working memory") and the subconscious mind ("hard wiring"). Or as W. Timothy Gallwey calls this, the "ten-cent computer" (the conscious mind) and the "million-dollar computer" (the subconscious mind).[7]

Any time we try a new activity, behavior, or way of thinking, we are literally forging a new pathway in our brain. We're creating circuits that don't currently exist. Doing this takes energy and focus, and requires extensive use of our conscious mind.

Imagine pouring huge amounts of data into a ten-cent computer, data that should be going through a supercomputer. Our circuits can easily overload, get confused, or freeze up. So the act of learning a new way of thinking or behaving is fraught with danger and uncertainty. We can't yet picture the new activity. Before we feel comfortable with an idea or behavior we have to own it, we have to develop our own hard wiring for the idea. Getting to this point requires we go through a stage of mild discomfort, uncertainty, and often even frustration and fear.

This concept has been widely studied within the field of change management, by people such as William Bridges and James Prochaska.[8] There is a model called the Phases of Change, which is useful to keep in mind when involved in any kind of change process. Let me illustrate this model with a story: Recently, a good friend joined me on a beach vacation and wanted me to help him learn how to surf.

For several days before we hit the water we talked excitedly about what it would be like to stand up on a wave. When we first jumped into the water, I immediately paddled out. Ten seconds later, already out past the breakers, I turned around to talk to my friend, assuming he'd be next to me. He was right where we'd jumped in, trying to paddle and immediately slipping off his board. I watched him do this about four times, then he suddenly got up, threw the board on the sand, and paced around. He'd just moved from phase one, unconscious incompetence, to phase two, conscious incompetence. This jump is often accompanied by strong negative emotions as people try activities they find out they don't know how to do, and get frustrated.

After a few days of practice he was able to paddle along okay, and toward the end of the week he was catching waves lying down. At one point he managed to get up on a wave and surf for about a second (I think it felt like a lifetime to him!). The energy generated by this brief moment filled our vacation house for the rest of the week. He had moved into the third phase, conscious competence— he'd been successful, though it required immense physical and mental energy.

While he was struggling in the water, I caught dozens of waves. I didn't have to think about surfing; it was a part of me. As we know now this is quite literally true—I had hardwired surfing into my brain.

How to make change more likely

So far we've seen that improving performance requires getting people to change, and that change can bring with it strong emotions. There are two things we can do here to help.

The first is to be aware that people often give up easily when they try something new, so it helps to let them know that their frustration is normal. Just as when my friend threw the board onto the sand, it can feel all too hard, so we stop. (He might have stopped had I not paddled back to shore to provide moral support.) Bear in mind that our brain is a finely tuned machine dedicated to protecting the status quo, and trying a new way of thinking or behaving can send alarm bells ringing, even bringing on the fight or flight response complete with an adrenaline rush. You sometimes see this when people's point of view is challenged. Understanding the phases that occur when we learn anything new, and letting people know what they are experiencing is normal, can help them stay the course. The technical term for this is "normalizing" someone's experience.

Second, given all the fear and uncertainty involved in creating any kind of new wiring, providing lots of positive feedback and encouragement can be a big help. We will explore this in more detail in a section coming up called "Accentuate the Positive."

Getting comfortable with encouraging discomfort

From an anthropological perspective it's pretty clear that human beings across the world like their creature comforts. A big chunk of the world's economy is built around reducing discomfort. Studies show that regular exercise can be a more effective depression fighter than antidepressants.[9] I am not attacking the health care professions here; my point is that millions of people are choosing to take a pill rather than do something that requires them to stretch themselves, to be uncomfortable. Much of the western world lives life with almost no physical exertion day to day, and one of the results is an epidemic of obesity. It's not that different from what happens when you put wild animals in a cage with an abundance of food and no exercise. We're eating ourselves to death, while doing everything we can to be more and more comfortable: buying bigger houses, softer beds, and cars built like lounge rooms.

As a society we not only want to be comfortable, we also have an unspoken conspiracy about not wanting to make anyone else uncomfortable, physically, mentally or emotionally. We're worried about losing friends, about upsetting people, about lawsuits. We'd much rather leave the status quo as it is. It's no wonder it's hard for leaders to improve performance, given this requires making people feel uncomfortable. It's almost on the level of a cultural taboo.

It's hard to stretch ourselves

Stretching seems to be an activity that is easier to do to another person than to ourselves. Why should we stretch ourselves, in areas where we don't feel comfortable? It goes against the warning signs our body and mind send us.

Most people have certain parts of their lives where they are comfortable feeling uncomfortable. Runners know they will feel a high after ten minutes of pushing past their pain; salespeople know if they can just face enough rejection they will get to a win and then feel great. But few people are willing to let themselves venture into the unknown across the board.

One of the difficulties of stretching ourselves is that we tend to see ourselves as our limitations, not as our potential. We're lost in our own world. Consider what happens when we start a new job. For the first few weeks, everything is exciting, but within six months we have settled into a level of sameness. After five years we're not likely to see a lot of potential when we walk into work in the mornings; we're going to see problems to solve, dramas to take care of, meetings to attend, and details to manage. When a new person comes in to start their first day, we're cynical about their fresh-faced enthusiasm.

You've been your own project your whole life, so by now you're a lot less excited about your own potential than someone who sees you with a fresher perspective. As we don't know what we're capable of, we tend to err on the side of caution; we set goals well within our capacity, goals that our mind can easily picture us achieving. My point here is it's hard to stretch ourselves, and most people spend their lives operating well within the bounds of what they are capable of achieving.

Why it works to stretch other people

I learned about the power of having someone else stretch us when I first took on a personal trainer a few years ago. I discovered an interesting pseudo-mathematical formula: that the difference between stretching myself and another person stretching me was infinite! My trainer got me doing exercises I would never have dreamed of, and then doing more repetitions than I could ever imagine, then repeating the process three times over. It was only during the second repetition that I realized I wasn't going to die, and I started to feel great. Would I have got there on my own? Definitely not. Having others stretch us is a way to grow faster than we would on our own.

The right amount of stretch

Think of a time you produced extraordinary results at work or in your personal life. For most people, these are times when we're being stretched. In his book *Flow*, scientist Mihaly Csikszentmihalyi proposes that the time we experience the strongest positive emotion comes from a zone in between boredom and anxiety.[10] Too much stretch equals stress, too little brings on boredom. He talks about a zone where we experience "flow"—an experience of just enough stretch, where we have to grow to achieve our goals, and we win often enough to stay inspired. I sense that most people are not operating within this zone at work. While many people in the workplace are stretched, it is through doing too much of the same thing. Their mental circuits start to get tired, just like any muscle does. Remember that learning occurs when people make new connections, when they develop insights in their own thinking, not just when they take on new knowledge. So stretch is about giving people a chance to use the knowledge they have in different ways, to develop their thinking along new lines, both figuratively and literally.

The right amount of stretch then is more about quality than quantity. It's stretching in different ways that generates new wiring. From what we learned about how different our brains all are, the right amount of stretch will be different for everyone. The best way to find out? Just ask.

In summary, Quiet Leaders don't just quietly putter around in the background trying not to upset anyone. They are comfortable making people uncomfortable—in fact, they're keen to do so. They know that stretch can be challenging; however, they have learned to support people through this journey. Above all they know that the right kind of stretch brings growth, and in growth there is aliveness, engagement, and passion, qualities that are necessary for achieving great performance in any role.

■ ■ ■ ■ ■ ■ ■ **EXERCISE STATION FOR** ■ ■ ■ ■ ■ ■ ■ ■

Remember to Stretch

This exercise will help you learn about stretch. Take a look at your schedule, and for every meeting you have planned, cut the time allocated to it to 25 percent of what you have allowed. In other words, if you've planned an hour meeting, allow just fifteen minutes. At the same time focus on achieving the same outcomes you intended in an hour. Make some notes below about what you notice.

_____

_____

_____

_____

_____

ACCENTUATE THE POSITIVE

If you treat an individual as he is, he will stay as he is,
but if you treat him as if he were what he ought to be and could be,
he will become what he ought and could be.

JOHANN WOLFGANG VON GOETHE (1749–1832)

PUT PROCESS BEFORE CONTENT
ACCENTUATE THE POSITIVE
REMEMBER TO STRETCH
FOCUS ON SOLUTIONS
LET THEM DO ALL THE THINKING

Figure 13, Accentuate the Positive

Quiet Leaders have a deep understanding of the absolute necessity of positive feedback to every human being.

At the start of a long overseas trip recently, I lost a pair of expensive glasses I had bought not that long before. Just after this trip, while delivering a workshop, I started talking about how often we criticize ourselves. In a flash I suddenly noticed my own thinking about my glasses. I took a moment to calculate how often I had been tough on myself and to my amazement it was around three hundred times over the month. Three hundred times I had said to myself, "Gosh you're an idiot." What a strange thing to do.

It turns out I am not more self-flagellating than most. I have asked thousands of people at workshops if they were their own worst critic. Except for a handful of people, who remarked that this was their mother's job, and just one woman who believed she was not, everyone else said they were extremely tough on themselves, tougher than anyone else.

When I have asked people to calculate the amount of self-criticism they experience, to total up the number of hours they are spending in this mental frame, the answer is quite remarkable. The lowest number anyone told me was five hundred hours a year, up to highs of over two thousand hours a year.

How much positive feedback does the average person get? Many human beings go months without any at all. For some this is the situation for years. From my own anecdotal research I estimate that on average, people get a couple of minutes each year of positive feedback, almost none of which is from themselves. And when they get it from others, they rarely let it in. Whereas they receive thousands of hours each year of criticism from themselves, as well as perceived criticism from others. We seem to be drowning in what we don't need, but it's a desert out there for what we do. I'm not talking about people with self-esteem problems or mental health issues. I am talking about successful executives, professionals, business owners, moms and dads, professors, politicians. We all seem to be in the same boat.

If you're wondering if maybe criticism is good for us, that it helps us perform better, consider some research that shows that employees reacted positively to criticism just once out of thirteen times.[11]

> Let me put this bluntly once more for the sake of clarity:
> People get, on average, a couple of minutes of positive feedback each year,
> versus thousands of hours of negative feedback.

Acknowledging that this is a reality for just about every human being you'll ever meet is a key step in learning to transform other people's performance. It's certainly something that all Quiet Leaders know, deep in their bones.

As the Iceberg model illustrated, back in Why Should Leaders

Care About Improving Thinking?, our performance is driven by our behaviors. Our behaviors are driven by our emotions, which are driven by our thinking. So our thinking is at the core of our performance. Yet we all have a lot of thoughts going on that are not supporting the performance we want. We are constantly criticizing, worrying, and imagining the worst. If we can help other people quiet this inner voice a little, we should be able to make a big difference to their thinking and therefore the results they produce.

This brings to mind what W. Timothy Gallwey did in the 1970s, coming out of his book *The Inner Game of Tennis*.[12] Tim declared he could teach anyone to play a game of tennis in only thirty minutes, using his special coaching techniques. A television station took him up on the challenge and supplied him with a middle-aged woman who hadn't exercised for decades and had never picked up a tennis racquet. I've seen the video and it's quite extraordinary. The woman comes onto the court and jokes around, clearly a little nervous. Tim asks her not to worry about hitting the ball at all, just to stand there however she felt comfortable and to watch the way the ball was spinning, left to right or the other way around. She didn't need to hit the ball at all unless she felt like it. He threw half a dozen balls and as she started to call out which way the ball was spinning he gave her lots of little encouragements. Then at one point she dropped her racquet down and hit the ball. As it happened, she hit it really well. This kept going for a while, and to her amazement, with no instruction and just by focusing on something else, she'd been able to work out on her own how to hit a decent forehand.

This goes on for thirty minutes of backhands, volleying, and serving, with Tim giving her different activities to focus on that gave her conscious mind something to do other than worrying. All the while he's giving her lots of positive feedback. True to his word, she plays a decent game of tennis with him after just thirty minutes of lessons. Yet he hardly gave her a single instruction during the whole process.

Out of this body of work came a formula I've found helpful over the years in improving my own performance. He said that our performance (p) equals our potential (P) minus our interference (I). In shorthand it's:

$$p = P - I$$

Tim saw clearly that people's fear, imagination, and self-doubt got in the way of their performance, and that underneath all of that we all had natural skills that if allowed to surface, would enable us to play quite well.

This story illustrates several principles of what a Quiet Leader does: Tim got his player to do the thinking rather than telling her how to play; he focused firmly on solutions; and he provided lots of positive feedback along the way, which made a big difference to her confidence and therefore her abilities.

Neuroscientist John Ratey has a theory for how our inner voice can stifle performance.[13] He believes that our neurons have limits to the amount of electrical signals they can process, and can therefore go into overload fairly easily. We always have a certain amount of ambient neural activity going on, even when we're asleep. When we experience anxiety, fear, self-consciousness or any strong emotion, our neurons get flooded with electrical signals, so there's not enough capacity left to process what is going on in the moment. We literally stop hearing and seeing what's around us.

Going back to the idea of a ten-cent versus a million-dollar computer, learning any new skill requires substantial neuronal activity until the skill we are practicing becomes hardwired into our subcortex. Given that we have a strong tendency to criticize ourselves, it's highly likely that these thoughts will be getting in the way of our performance much of the time. Therefore acknowledgment and encouragement from others will help calm our mind, and allow us to focus on what we are trying to achieve. Or in the language of the brain, positive feedback leaves our neurons free to focus where they're needed most.

Significant research has been done on the impact of positive feedback on children's development, their IQ, and their well-being.[14] It's not just that everyone knows intellectually that children need positive feedback; I believe it's hard coded into us to provide it. My evidence is shared, I'm sure, by most new fathers: Since the moment my daughter was born, no complex conversation could happen within a twenty foot radius of her—everyone was too engrossed in giving her positive feedback.

We seem to have decided that once people become adults they don't need positive feedback. I'm not so sure. I was about to show a colleague some draft pages of this book. I knew that if the writing excited her, I would have a much better day than if she didn't like it. Feedback has an impact on me. And lots of research is showing it has a big impact on performance across the board.[15]

If we want to transform people's performance we need to master the skill of acknowledgment. This means building new mental wiring around seeing what people are doing well. It means watching out for how people are challenging themselves, growing, learning, and developing. And it means noticing the new wiring others are developing, and being able to feed back what we see in ways that make a difference.

This can be harder than it sounds, especially for hard-edged leaders. Some executives don't want to give people positive feedback. They worry it could make people complacent, or worse, want to ask for a promotion. Many of these leaders are highly competitive alpha males who've climbed their way to the top by stepping on others on the way up. For these people, giving positive feedback could be quite a new concept. Yet I can't see any leader being capable of consistently bringing out the best in others without this skill.

One organization that has embraced the concept of positive feedback as part of their culture is IBM. I spent two days at their head office in upstate New York in 2004, doing some work with their global team of facilitators. I noticed people there would go out of their way to congratulate each other for their achievements, something I hadn't seen in the workplace before. Perhaps part of IBM's success is that good people don't want to leave because they get more recognition than they get anywhere else.

Another implication of the whole principle of Accentuate the Positive is that we need to learn a new model for giving feedback in the workplace. If people are their own worst critics—giving themselves too much criticism as it is—maybe they don't need anyone else jumping on the bandwagon. Currently the main way of giving feedback is to explore "what you did well, and what you could do better." To people who are tough on themselves, which is basically everyone, all they hear is what they did wrong.

There are nifty ways of trying to pretend that you're doing something else, called a "feedback sandwich" in which you hide the "meat" (what they did wrong) inside two bits of positive feedback, hoping it won't hurt as much. I propose this is just a manipulative way of trying to disguise that we're going to talk about what people did wrong. Of course, compared to just blurting out negative feedback, a feedback sandwich is an improvement. But so is putting deck chairs in neat rows on a boat about to sink.

If we want to transform people's performance, we need a new model for feedback that's not just new packaging of the same thing. A new approach would follow these types of questions:

What did you do well, and what did you discover about yourself as a result?
What were the highlights of this project and what did you learn?
What went well and would you like to talk about how to do more of this?
What did you do well and what impact do you think this had on everyone else?

I am not saying we should gloss over the facts if a person completely messes up; there are times for honest and direct conversations about poor performance. I am proposing that because people are so tough on themselves, and because it works better to focus on creating new wiring than solving problems, that overall we will be better at improving performance if we accentuate the positive and let people handle the negative on their own.

Marshall Goldsmith formalized this idea into a technique he calls FeedForward.[16] With FeedForward, instead of discussing an issue that didn't work well in the past, we discuss what we'd like to change in the future, and explore ways to make this possible. Now that you understand the way the brain works, it's clear why this type of approach is more effective than discussing our problems. We will come back to this whole idea toward the end of the book in a chapter about giving feedback in any type of situation.

Here's a few examples of how a Quiet Leader might accentuate the positive.

Appreciation:	I really appreciate you completing that report on time.
Validation:	I can see you've given this report a lot of thought and attention.
Recognition:	It's clear you are a very talented writer.
Affirmation:	I think you deserve all the credit for this project.
Confirmation:	It's great you took on this project, it suited your style.
Thanking:	Thanks for taking the time to focus 100 percent on this project.

A new idea?

It's probably not the first time you've heard that positive feedback is important. Ken Blanchard captured this idea brilliantly in one of the world's best-selling business books, *The One Minute Manager*,[17] where he talks about catching people doing things right. However, knowing you *should* give more positive feedback is not the same as doing it. If you think all these principles are basic—it's true, they are. That doesn't mean they are easy to live by. What's required here is the creation of new wiring.

In summary, Quiet Leaders know that transforming performance requires providing continuous positive feedback, in many forms, over time. To validate, confirm, encourage, support, and believe in people's potential. As people begin to see themselves in a new light, reality starts to change as well.

■ ■ ■ ■ ■ ■ ■ **EXERCISE STATION FOR** ■ ■ ■ ■ ■ ■ ■ ■

Accentuate the Positive

Giving people positive feedback can be a deeply rewarding exercise as it feels great for both parties and deepens our connections with people. As an exercise to start with, practice acknowledging yourself. Pay attention to what you've done well, the challenges you surmounted, the fears you stared down, or how you pushed past an obstacle that would normally stop you. Choose one main thing every day for at least three days to acknowledge yourself for. You could do this at the end of the day before you sleep as a way to put you in a nice frame of mind to rest.

Next, move on to practicing acknowledging other people. You could start off with finding one different person every day to acknowledge. It's as simple as noticing carefully what people are doing. Acknowledgment should be more than just saying, "You're great!" It's about noticing what people do and how they make a difference. It's useful to be as specific as you can.

PUT PROCESS BEFORE CONTENT

Before anything else, preparation is the key to success.

ALEXANDER GRAHAM BELL (1847–1922)

Figure 14, Put Process Before Content

Imagine an up-and-coming professional tennis player having a conversation with his or her coach at the start of the season. One of the most important things they do each year is set specific goals, plans, and milestones for the road ahead. Without these, it would be difficult to track progress, therefore hard to give positive feedback or know what to focus on at any moment.

At the macro level, having "good process" means having clear objectives each year to focus on. At the micro level, good process means that every time you have a conversation to improve a person's performance, you plan for the success of the dialogue itself. This includes establishing clear expectations so that at every moment you both know exactly what you are talking about, and why, and where you are trying to get to.

By establishing good process for dialogues, before getting lost in the details of a conversation, you are more likely to have discussions that are *useful* rather than just *interesting*.

Examples of good process in a conversation

- You both know what your roles are in the dialogue.
- You both know how long you plan to speak.
- You both know and agree on the outcome you are trying to achieve in the conversation.
- You both know how this conversation ties in to other issues such as overall goals.
- You both understand explicitly where you are coming from in the conversation.
- You choose the specific type of thinking approach most likely to work in any moment. For example, using a brainstorming process to develop ideas.
- You constantly clarify the main points of the dialogue, to help keep you both focused on the core issues.

All of these are examples of how to make sure a conversation has the best chance of success. Remember that any time you want someone's brain to do something new it is likely to bring up fear and concern, stopping their neurons from processing new ideas. So it's important to make people feel safe.

Much of the last two steps in this book, Dance Toward Insight and Create New Thinking, are about good process in dialogues, so I am not going to go into detail on the "how" of this just yet, except for one specific model that's one of my favorites.

Choose Your Focus

I have a model to bring the concept of Process before Content alive called the Choose Your Focus model. This is one of the most popular ideas I have developed in the last few years, though it's also the simplest one. The simplicity of this model allows us to remember it more easily, which makes it even more useful.

The Choose Your Focus model helps people orient their thought processes. It helps us identify the type of thinking we are doing at any moment, and provides an opportunity to then choose where to put our focus. This tool can be useful before any type of difficult conversation, for team meetings, or any time you are tackling a difficult thinking task.

How Choose Your Focus was developed

At the start of an annual review of an operation a few years ago, it became clear that there was a lot of potential for conflict in the day ahead. We'd packed a lot of big ideas into one day: setting goals for the year ahead, developing strategies, making some tough decisions, as well as managing lots of details. A number of these issues also contained the potential for emotional charge within them.

As we started the day I realized that if we didn't consciously choose how to structure the conversation we could easily end up not getting through our agenda. In an instant I pictured that there were five different "flavors" of conversation we could have at any moment, and that it was going to work best if we started from the top down. By managing the day this way we had a highly productive meeting, without the focus on problems we could have had. From that point on I have been teaching this tool widely, and people seem to love it.

About the model

The Choose Your Focus model says there are five different ways we can think about, or communicate about, any project, whether the project is a merger, a cultural change process, a sales target at work, or just a one-on-one meeting. The model helps us recognize which gear we are thinking from, and then allows us to actively choose another way to think. The five levels are:

1. **Vision:** *Vision thinking* is about the "why" or "what." Why do you want to do this project? What are you trying to achieve?

What's your goal here? Having a clear vision is about knowing what your goal or objective is in any given conversation or project.

2. **Planning:** Once you know where you are heading, *planning thinking* is about how you're going to get there. Putting in place good planning, without worrying about the details yet, is an excellent way of ensuring the success of any idea.

3. **Detail:** Once we know where we're going, and how we're going to get there, we need to take action. *Detail thinking* is simply that—the detail of doing. Detail is where people tend to naturally put most of their energy unless they step back and think about how they are approaching what they are doing.

4. **Problem:** *Problem thinking* is the territory of events going wrong. Focusing on problems is unfortunately a common experience in business, as there are lots of them. However, it's possible to focus on problems without coming from a problem-focus. For example, you could tackle a problem from a vision perspective, or from a planning perspective.

5. **Drama:** *Drama thinking* is the place where the vision, planning, detail, and problems have fallen apart and all that is left is emotional charge. Sometimes it's unavoidable that you spend time in this mental state—for example, in a grieving process you might be unable to do much as your emotions have taken

Figure 15, Choose Your Focus

over. Unfortunately, drama is a place where many people in organizations are stuck and find it hard to get out of on their own.

This model is so simple you can easily reproduce the concepts in any conversation. I often do this by writing it down on paper or putting it up on a whiteboard, for people to see the concept for themselves. The most common impact of this model is that people notice themselves lost in details, not clear on *what* they are trying to achieve, or *how*.

Imagine you are trying to help someone come up with a title for a new product, such as choosing the title for this book. A common way to do this is to sit down and come up with ideas, and then debate all the good and bad points about each title. It's fairly likely you won't get to a great outcome going this way. If you used the Choose Your Focus model you might start off with questions like:

What's your goal for the title itself?
What do you want the title to say?

You might then see that you want the title to be memorable, sharp, and speak of something that everyone can relate to.

Once you knew the vision for the project, a great next question would be a planning question, such as: "What do you think you need to do to come up with the right title? What process might work here?"

In this case, you might decide that you needed to list twenty existing titles you liked, map out the major possible directions the title could go, and make a list of one hundred possible titles from there. If you followed a process like this, taking one step at a time, when you got to the detail phase it would be much easier, and there's less chance of problems or dramas.

Quiet Leaders are highly disciplined in their conversations. They are diligently focused on ensuring every conversation is as productive as possible every step of the way, and if it's not, they do something about this. They know that it's important to get the process of any conversation right before getting into any of the content of a dialogue.

■ ■ ■ ■ ■ ■ ■ **EXERCISE STATION FOR** ■ ■ ■ ■ ■ ■ ■

Put Process Before Content

You can do this exercise on your own, though you might like to talk to a partner or friend about it, to help make the process more tangible.

Think of three projects you are working on right now. Then take a look at this model and pinpoint where your thinking is right now in each project. It would be even more effective to write this down.

Once you know which level you are thinking on around each project, think about where would be the most useful level to focus on at the moment. If you are lost in the details, should you be spending time in planning phase? If you are lost in all the problems of the project, do you need to revisit the vision of why you are doing it? Take time to rethink your own thinking about your projects here.

_____

_____

_____

_____

_____

_____

_____

_____

Let's summarize the entire first step to being a Quiet Leader, which is to think about thinking. Quiet Leaders let other people do all the thinking, then gently keep the conversation focused on solutions. They stretch people more than people stretch themselves, while providing extensive positive feedback. And they know that taking time to establish good process in any situation is a key to having the most useful conversations. Having all these ideas in mind is the first step to being able to improve people's thinking without telling them what to do. It's the first step to transforming performance at work.

■ STEP 2 ■

LISTEN FOR POTENTIAL

---

*The future belongs to people who see possibilities
before they become obvious.*

TED LEVITT (CIRCA 1990)

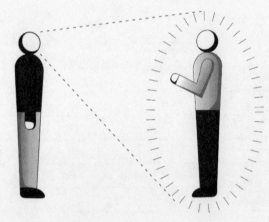

Figure 16, Listen for Potential

Imagine you're at a friend's birthday party, we'll call her Ming. Ming's parents are there, as are several of her friends including an accountant, a lawyer, an executive search consultant, a car salesman, a doctor, and a psychologist. At the end of a long lunch Ming says: "I've been thinking a lot lately about getting a better job. Work's been getting me down, and I think I could make more money if I bought a car and got into sales."

What would these people say to the birthday girl?

The parents might say something like: *"Oh dear, we're sorry it's not worked out, we know you've been working hard there, we wish you'd just take better care of yourself . . ."*

The accountant might say something like: *"You might find that after taxes are taken into account you're no better off."*

The lawyer might say something like: *"Did they give you a proper job specification in your contract? Could you sue them for withholding information?"*

The executive search consultant might say something like: *"I might know someone who could use you. Why don't you come down and see me this week?"*

The doctor might say something like: *"Sounds like you're under a bit of stress there. Have you been sleeping okay?"*

The car salesman might say something like: *"Great idea—there's a lot of money in sales. Give me a call and we can chat about ideas for your new car."*

The psychologist might say something like: *"Have you thought about talking to someone about your problems at work?"*

I know I am making some generalizations here, but play along with me for a moment. Even though most of these people want to help Ming, I doubt they're being all that helpful. Partly this is because everyone is simply giving advice, but it's something else as well. Everyone has their own filter, agenda, or emotional hot spot (three ideas I will illustrate further in this chapter). They are not listening to Ming as someone capable, strong, and fully able to come up with great ideas and solutions. They are listening to her as someone in difficulty who needs their help. Which of these is right: Does Ming need help, or does she have the answers inside her?

The answer, it turns out, is that both perspectives are correct. It depends on what you believe to be true. Let's go back to the neuroscience here. Even before any data from the outside world enters our brain, our neurons are primed to seek out certain bits of information based on the various mental frames we hold.[18] This goes back to the insight about the brain that our hard wiring drives automatic perceptions.

It turns out—and this is based in scientific research—that we literally only hear what we listen for. We pay special attention to what we are expecting to see, hear, feel, or taste. As Jeff Hawkins says,

> "What we perceive is a combination of what we sense and of our brains' memory-derived predictions . . . 'Prediction' means that the neurons involved in sensing become active in advance of actually receiving sensory input. When the sensory input does arrive, it is compared with what was expected . . . Prediction is not just one of the things your brain does. It is the primary function of the neocortex, and the foundation of intelligence." [19]

Or as Jeffrey Schwartz says, "not only do mental states matter to the physical activity of the brain, but they can contribute to the final perception even more powerfully than the stimulus itself." [20] In other words, when you listen to people, unless you consciously choose a certain way to listen, you will listen to prove your existing theories about this person. This is hardly the most effective way of transforming performance.

So what is the most effective way to actively listen to people, to maximize their performance? To answer this question I'd like to offer you an opportunity to develop some insights yourself instead of just giving you my answer.

■ ■ ■ ■ ■ ■ ■ **EXERCISE STATION FOR** ■ ■ ■ ■ ■ ■ ■

Noticing How I Listen

Go and speak to someone for a few minutes. Anyone. Use the phone if nobody is around. While you are listening to them, notice what else you are listening to while they speak. Or said another way, what other thoughts do you notice running around inside your head while you are listening?

Here's a list of what you might have noticed going on. It's not a complete list, but these tend to be the common approaches to listening. Check the approaches that you found yourself doing.

❏ Listening for opportunities to sound intelligent
❏ Listening for a chance to seem funny
❏ Listening for how you can sound important
❏ Listening to get information you want
❏ Listening to external distractions such as other noises, music, etc.
❏ Listening for what's going on with the other person
❏ Listening to your own thoughts, and not listening at all
❏ Listening to see how you can help
❏ Listening to understand the problem
❏ Listening for how you can benefit

Now that you have checked a few of the boxes, what do you notice? Take a moment to make some notes for yourself.

Insights I Got from Noticing How I Listen to People

_____

_____

_____

_____

_____

I have put hundreds of people from many different cultures through exercises similar to this. The first thing people tend to notice is that they really only listen a small percentage of the time, with the rest of their attention being put to judging, assessing, trying to sound smart, listening to distractions, trying to size other people up, or being self-conscious to the point that they are only in fact listening to themselves.

So we still have this question to answer: What is the most effective way to listen to people, when you want them to perform at their best? Try to answer this before reading any further.

The most common responses people give me are "active listening," or "listening for what people feel," or "listening for what the problem is" or something similar. While these styles of listening are probably more useful than not listening fully, or listening for a chance to be funny, they are still limited in comparison to what's possible. There is, in fact, a whole other way.

A NEW WAY TO LISTEN

What would a Quiet Leader say to Ming about her challenges at work? He or she might say: "Sounds exciting! This could be a great opportunity to take some time to think about what you really want from a career, a chance to reinvent your future."

You could say that Quiet Leaders are just optimists, and while this is partially true, Quiet Leaders do far more than just see the bright side to every dark cloud. A Quiet Leader does a critical thing—they listen for people's potential. When a Quiet Leader listens, they listen to people and believe in others completely. They encourage and support others in being the best they can be, just in how they listen, without saying a word. They listen to people as though they have all the tools they need to be successful, and could simply benefit from exploring their thoughts and ideas out loud.

Examples of listening for potential

Imagine you're at a weekly team meeting with your direct reports and someone you are managing says: "I'm not sure what to do about this project." If you were listening for potential you might say something like the following:

How can I best help you think this through?
Do you want to use me as a sounding board?
Do you have a sense of what you want to do, and want to explore that with me?

The assumption we make behind these questions is that people have the answers and we're just here to help them think.

Or someone says: "I feel like I made a mess of that project." If you were listening for potential you might say something such as, "Sounds like you're having a rough time. What have you learned from taking on this client so far?"

As you can see, there are many different words you can use, there's no one cookie-cutter approach for exactly what to say when you're listening this way. When you listen for potential, you're assuming that others have the capacity to answer the question for themselves; you then respectfully see how you can best make yourself useful.

Listening for potential is a choice in every moment. By choosing to listen to people as successful, competent, and able to resolve their own dilemmas, guess what's likely to happen? They often solve their own problems, and get on with the job.

When I ask people in workshops to try listening this way, something magical happens. They report that their internal chatter becomes almost nonexistent. They find themselves seeing the other person in a new way, becoming fascinated by what they have to say. They find themselves being very present and in the moment, and, above all, having a much better time as they listen. And listen they do—reporting that the majority of their attention goes into listening deeply when they are listening for potential.

Quiet Leaders listen for potential. They understand that if we're not measuring and monitoring how people are growing, we can easily fall into the trap of focusing on their problems. They know that the first step to seeing positive change in others is to expect it.

■ ■ ■ ■ ■ ■ ■ EXERCISE STATION FOR ■ ■ ■ ■ ■ ■ ■

Listen for Potential

Go and talk with someone you speak with a lot. It doesn't matter if it's face to face, or by telephone, or across the back fence—just talk to someone you know, and ask them how their week has been. While they speak, listen for their strengths, for what they are passionate about, for whom they could become, for what their potential is, not just who or what they are. And just see what happens.

_____

_____

_____

_____

_____

THE CLARITY OF DISTANCE

Science creates a power through its knowledge, a power to do things.
You are able to do things after you know something scientifically.

RICHARD FEYNMAN (1964)

Listening for potential requires a willingness to identify and put aside mental states that could cloud our ability to listen openly. This brings us to my second most favorite model, the Clarity of Distance.

This model came to me after noticing something quite unexpected. While I was running different exercises among small groups in my workshops, I found that the less involved in a situation I was, the more I was able to see what was really going on. When I had distance from an issue, I could recognize the patterns more easily.

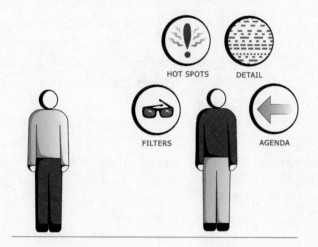

Figure 17, The Clarity of Distance

It's like my natural intelligence increased substantially when I wasn't too close. Malcolm Gladwell talks about a similar concept in his book *Blink,* where he shows how our immediate responses from afar are often significantly more on the mark than any number of hours of painstaking analysis of a situation.[21] Over time I found there were four mental frames that seemed to get in the way of my natural clarity, which I summarized as details, filters, agendas, and hot spots.

The Clarity of Distance model helps us to identify what's getting in the way of our natural intelligence, so that we can then go back to listening for potential. It's a model with broad application that can make a big difference to our self-awareness and therefore our ability to impact others.

Let me give you a little more background to this concept. Leaders and scientists have a lot in common. They both want to find patterns within seemingly chaotic systems in order to further understand and therefore have some control over those systems. In order to study anything in science you first must have an observer. The observer watches events unfold and seeks knowledge and understanding. The observer can't be the same as the event; there needs to be separation between the two.

In the Clarity of Distance model, there are four mental frames we can be stuck in that mean we lose our natural clarity. When we are stuck in one of these frames, we're too close—we've lost our distance, we are no longer an observer. The result is that no science, or great leadership, can occur.

When you have lost your natural clarity, the first step to going back to listening for potential is to identify what has sent you off course, and then refocus back on the person you are speaking with. Let's take a look at the elements of this model now.

Lost in the details

Every day at work is full of massive amounts of information, and with everything moving so quickly we have little time to reflect. As a result, many people spend a lot of time during the day lost in the *details*, unclear about which direction they should be going at any moment.

Listening to people as their potential requires that we stay above the details; otherwise we get lost in the tangled forest of information and can't see what's going on. We need to be the guide standing on a platform above the trees, who can see the qualities of the forest itself, notice the pathways, and therefore help our people find their way through. If we're lost too, we're not much help.

Here's an example. Saul is a production manager at a large plastics factory. He just had a rough week, pulling late nights to get a job done on deadline. You're sitting down to have a conversation with Saul the following week, and your intent is to help him make sure this doesn't happen again. However, by asking Saul what happened, you hear a blow-by-blow account of what went on including the details of each project, how late he stayed each night, even what type of pizza he ordered at 2:00 a.m. Is any of this information going to help you help Saul? I doubt it—in fact, quite the opposite. Wouldn't it be better to say something such as "I'd like to be a useful sounding board for you. How can I best help you learn from last week, without getting into the details?" Saul's answer might then be "Well, it would be worthwhile looking at what resources I am allowed to draw on next time." Now, without having to get detailed, you can be a big help to Saul, and quickly too.

I'm sure you've experienced being lost in the details yourself. When you notice you're lost, you can always remember the Choose Your Focus model and step up to vision thinking ("What was our objective in speaking today, again?") or planning thinking ("How long did we plan to spend on this first issue?"). Usually just realizing we are lost in the details is enough to help us to get back on track.

Misled by our filters

Filters are the unconscious mental frames through which we see, the sum of our assumptions, expectations, predictions, and decisions about anything. Going back to the birthday party, Ming's parents listen the way most parents do, out of general concern for their loved ones. The doctor listens through concern for Ming's physical well-being, the lawyer listens from a legal perspective, and the psychologist listens to see if Ming's mental health is okay.

There's nothing wrong with having filters—they're an important part of our makeup. Filters help us predict situations without having to process enormous amounts of data. The challenge with filters is we tend to be unconscious of them, and as we learned early on, we then do our best to make the world fit into the way we think it is.

When our filters are accurate, such as the filter "Electric stove burners are hot when they are red," that's helpful. However, as leaders we've developed filters for most of the people we manage, filters we're no longer conscious of, and often these are based on incomplete or inaccurate assumptions. As a result, we're now listening to people according to decisions we made about them some time ago. Going back to the conversation with Saul, if we had the filter that he was always goofing off at work, we'd assume he wasn't really working when he was there late at night. In this case it would be difficult to have a conversation and listen for his potential.

Being misled by our filters is the second most common trap when we listen to others. When we listen through filters, we are fitting people into our predetermined boxes, rather than helping them be all they could be. Like with the other elements of the Clarity of Distance model, the fastest way to step back into a more effective way to listen is to identify the filter you have, and actively choose to listen in a new way.

Having an agenda

Several people at Ming's party had quite clear agendas. Especially the executive search consultant and the car salesman, who both see opportunities to benefit financially from Ming's situation. An agenda clouds our ability to listen to people as their potential. We're suddenly too close, we're lost in our own agenda instead of seeing the other person's possibilities.

When you manage someone you naturally have lots of agendas going on. You might want them to succeed so that you look good as their manager. You might want them to fit into the team. You want them to perform, to deliver. Or you might not want them to be more successful than you. All of these agendas can cloud your ability to bring out the best in your people.

Identifying an agenda is the key to being able to put it to one side. Sometimes declaring your agenda out loud can help here. I can remember saying the statement below many times when I was driving the sales of our training programs in the past: "I obviously have an agenda here, which is that I want to see the sales improve, but I am going to put that aside and see how I can best help you think through the week ahead."

Hot spots

Going back to Ming's situation, if you'd recently lost your job unexpectedly and were unhappy about it, you would have a *hot spot*, a mental frame that would make it hard to listen to Ming's story without bringing your own emotional charge to the table. A hot spot is a charged issue for us, an issue that we're lost in the emotions of. Going back to the Choose Your Focus model, when we have a hot spot we tend to be lost in the *drama* of a situation—we're engaged emotionally. It's beyond just a problem.

In Daniel Goleman's book *Emotional Intelligence*,[22] he tells the story of how our more primitive brain takes over during certain situations and we literally do stop listening to our usual, higher order intelligence. We act impulsively, doing things that we wouldn't normally do.

When you're trying to listen to someone as their potential and the conversation results in either of you tripping over a hot spot, there's not much you can do. The best course of action could be to head home for the day; once our emotions are engaged it takes several hours to settle down and be able to think straight again. Broaching a charged issue another time may be a better use of resources.

In summary, we all have the ability to listen to other people as their potential. However, it's also easy to get lost in the details, misled by our filters and agendas, or sidetracked by our hot spots. It's a matter of understanding these frames and being aware of where you are coming from when you are listening to others. Once we become aware of what is clouding our natural clarity, we are on the way to listening to people in a whole new way.

Having the clarity of distance means having a state of mind where nothing is in the way of improving people's performance. Quiet Leaders know that listening for people's potential takes effort at times, and are conscious of what takes them off this course.

■ ■ ■ ■ ■ ■ ■ ■ **EXERCISE STATION FOR** ■ ■ ■ ■ ■ ■ ■ ■

The Clarity of Distance

The outcome of this exercise should be that you are able to distinguish your own mental states, and have more control over how you listen to other people. I suggest doing this with either a close friend or partner. You might get some unexpected side benefits from doing the exercise, too.

Write the following four words nice and big and leave them somewhere you will see them often during the week, for example on the fridge, on your computer desktop, or every day in your diary:

Detail
Filter
Agenda
Hot spots

Over the next three days, make a tally of the number of times you notice both yourself and other people speaking from one of these places. This can be at home, at work, anywhere. At the end of the three days, tally up the numbers for each area and see what you notice.

Insights I Got from Noticing
What Gets in the Way of Listening for Potential

_____

_____

_____

_____

_____

SPEAK WITH INTENT

Finding colleagues who, like lovers and friends, are inspiring rather than boring or dominating is increasingly a priority.

THEODORE ZELDIN (2002)

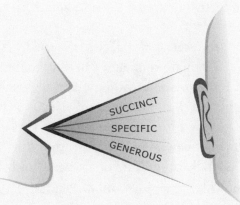

Figure 18, Speak with Intent

We've now completed the first two steps toward transforming performance as a Quiet Leader. We know that Quiet Leaders think about thinking and they listen for potential. In step three we explore what it takes to speak so that you have the maximum possible likelihood of improving people's thinking. This concept is particularly relevant in our communication-saturated world.

Imagine if our Internet protocols, the rules for how two computers share ideas, worked only 66 percent of the time. What would we be doing about it? When it comes to sharing ideas between people, my hunch is that we're at about that same efficiency: our ideas are being received by the other person in the way they are intended about two thirds of the time. The impact of our conversation is in some way different from our intent. *Intent versus impact* is another two-part construct we will come back to throughout the book.

As an outsider to organizations, I see with a fresh eye, I have the clarity of distance. To me the quality of day-to-day conversations in many workplaces is excruciatingly low. I have watched teams spend weeks discussing ideas that could have been decided on in minutes. I've seen leaders not saying what they really mean, and therefore others misunderstanding their intentions and reacting to ideas that no one even voiced. Suddenly we have all these unnecessary conversations flying around, taking up our valuable and increasingly stretched thinking time.

Having poor conversational skills will get you by, day to day, but a whole other level of skill is required if you want to transform people's performance. It reminds me of riding a bicycle when I was young. While hanging out on the street with my friends, it was fine to ride around casually, paying little attention to what I was doing. But if I was hurtling down a freeway at 50 mph with traffic on either side I needed to have a whole other level of attention and skill, or the day could get bad quickly. And once things went wrong, there was no turning back.

In this delicate and very human conversation called transforming performance, with strong emotions lurking just beneath the surface, if what we are trying to say is even slightly misunderstood, our conversations can go off the rails fast. To me it's clear why many managers don't give a lot of feedback—they're afraid of causing accidents.

Over a few years of coaching people to communicate more clearly, I noticed three core patterns that get in the way. The first was that people took much longer than necessary to describe their ideas. As a result, the listener often "checked out" of the conversation. They'd be waiting so long to speak, the result was a series of monologues rather than a dialogue. The second was the listener not understanding exactly what the speaker was saying. So conversations would go off on sidetracks, resulting in the intent of a conversation not being achieved. The third pattern was that the speaker didn't speak in language and concepts the listener could immediately grasp. As a result, the conversation became a debate about the meaning of words and ideas, instead of focusing on the real issues. Let's take a look at each of these three patterns now.

BE SUCCINCT

When there is a gap between one's real and declared aims,
one turns instinctively to long words and exhausted idioms,
like cuttlefish squirting out ink.

GEORGE ORWELL (1903–1950)

We speak on average at one hundred words per minute, but think at much higher rates, about six hundred words per minute.[23] So to create real change in others we first must capture and keep people's attention. We need to be in a focused dialogue, not speaking while the other person mentally wanders off.

Being succinct engages people in the conversation you'd like to have. There are two reasons for this. First, focusing on being succinct makes the speaker get clearer about their core message, before they speak. This in itself means their conversations will be more focused. They might complete a message in a couple of sentences instead of a few minutes. For the listener, the conversation is also far more engaging when the speaker is more authentic. As Lao-tzu said, "Sincere words are not embellished; embellished words are not sincere."

Second, being succinct provides the listener with a chance to process bite-sized pieces of information, rather than having to digest several minutes of ideas at once. We want people to feel confident inside any difficult dialogues, but our working memory isn't very big, and our ten-cent computer can be easily flummoxed.

Going back to the science here, when we speak, we want the person we're speaking with to generate maps in their own mind about what we are saying, and then to compare these to their existing maps, so that they might make connections between the two. Given how complex our brains are, the more simply, and above all, more clearly we can describe our thoughts to others, the more chance these connections might occur.

Being succinct saves significant time and mental energy. When we're succinct we use less time to get across our ideas, the other person understands our ideas more quickly, and there is less debate about any points that were not clear. This leaves us the time and mental energy to go deeper into topics, or to move to a new issue. While it might take a bit of additional energy up front, the benefits of being succinct are immediate and tangible.

Let's look at two different ways that you might describe an upcoming meeting to a colleague:

> We're having a big meeting next Monday about our targets, we want to decide if we're going to reach them or not. Richard's coming in to present the report from last quarter on sales compared to actuals from last year, it's important to see where we are in comparison. We need to take a look at the two years carefully and see what the difference is, if the sales we're doing this quarter are much different from last year, and in what way they are different. It will be useful to do some comparisons, check out all the variables and define exactly what's changed and what's stayed the same.

This is an example of one of those all too common "too much information" moments when we mentally check out. The person was going on and on about the same topic, getting more detailed than necessary. They were taking the same point and saying it over and over in different ways. They took the same single idea and then tried to show lots of angles on it . . . and what do you know, I am doing it now.

So what happens when someone is not succinct, like toward the end of my last paragraph? Did you feel spoken down to? Bored? Frustrated? What do you do as a result? Most of us have very short attention spans, though we rarely admit this to others or to ourselves. I personally find that when people start to waffle, a part of me stops listening. Waffling is like an unconscious signal for "what I am saying is not true so don't bother listening too carefully."

Let's make that last example more succinct:

> We're having a big meeting next Monday to carefully review how we are doing this quarter compared to last year. It's an important meeting so make sure you prepare thoroughly for it.

This example gets the information across but is easier to digest and therefore going to be more useful to the listener.

I was running a workshop on this concept for a technology firm recently. It was a room full of smart people who felt they were excellent communicators. I asked a well-dressed gentleman named Mario one of my favorite questions: "What will it take for you to be really succinct when you communicate?"

Mario responded with this: "I don't know, I guess I am happy talking, I don't pay attention to whether the other person is really connected with me, he could be focusing elsewhere and I wouldn't know it. So I should pay more attention, by being more focused, maybe I should focus on what the person's face is doing, then I might get distracted by their features as I like looking at how people's faces are laid out, it's an interest I have, but overall I think it would be useful if I looked at the other person more, maybe sized up how they sit, look at the way they look at me. I could read their body language and . . ." I asked permission to cut him off at this point. Suddenly Mario's face broke into a smile. "I wasn't very succinct, was I?" he asked.

With Mario's okay, I asked the group to define the place when they'd heard enough to understand his point. The unanimous response was after these words: "I don't pay attention to whether the other person is really connected with me," the first sentence Mario had spoken.

"So you're saying I should cut my statements down to one sentence?" Mario asked.

"Well, sometimes," I responded, "if that's enough for people to truly get your message, which it very often is."

"Wow, to do that I would have to stop and take a moment to actually think," Mario replied. The room reacted with a big laugh and several people clapped, acknowledging Mario for his succinctness.

The power of visuals

When I ask people how they become more succinct, one of the common responses I get points to the science around this idea. An easy way to be more succinct is to "picture" in your own mind what you are trying to say, and then use visual words and metaphor to get across what you see. By doing this, we are connecting with our own mental maps, then helping other people make their own mental maps for our ideas. Given that the brain processes ideas fastest visually,[24] this means that information can be shared between people much faster.

Compare the impact of these two ways of saying the same thing:

We want to take the time to invest more money in the business units on the West Coast, which we put in place last year, to give them a chance to develop. We knew then that it would take a few years to get good returns, and why should we be impatient and move our funds to investing in new sites when we haven't given the original sites enough resources yet? It will be more efficient to give these people more resources now than to open new sites.

We want to water the seeds we have already planted, rather than sow new fields.

Did you understand the concept I was trying to say earlier, more clearly? Could you see a field in your mind when you read the second example? If so, perhaps you now have your own mental map of what

I mean when I say that using visuals draws listeners in and allows them to make their own mental maps of your ideas.

In summary, being succinct requires you to think, to decide quickly on the essence of what you want to say, and say it in as few words as possible, focusing on using visual words. By cutting to the heart of the issue, you keep people's attention and interest. This allows people to make their own mental models that correlate to the ideas you are trying to share. When we're trying to transform performance, given that we know this will only happen if people have insights for themselves, giving people the space to create their own mental maps of our ideas is an essential first step to change.

■ ■ ■ ■ ■ ■ ■ **EXERCISE STATION FOR** ■ ■ ■ ■ ■ ■ ■ ■

Be Succinct

Practice explaining yourself in single sentences for one day. Or if you prefer, focus on halving the number of words you use. Try this out in all sorts of situations and see what happens. Write down your insights from doing this exercise, as clearly as you can, as an exercise in being succinct in itself. Summarize the insights you uncover about being succinct—in succinct, visual sentences. For example, "I can see that people listen more when I am succinct," or "I can be more succinct with a little focus."

_____

_____

_____

_____

_____

_____

_____

BE SPECIFIC

The challenge of using simple language is
you have to know what you are talking about.

The *New York Times* on the Italian government's
attempts to simplify their language (2002)

At the same time as using as few words as possible, we still need to be specific enough so that people understand exactly what we mean. We need to provide just enough information to illustrate the point we are making; otherwise the conversation could end up on unnecessary sidetracks.

Imagine that you are completing a meeting with a new staff member. Saying "That was a great meeting" may not have much impact; it might even be perceived as glib or insincere. Compare that to this more specific response: "That was a great meeting—especially the way we were able to bounce ideas off each other, and how easy it was to get through such a big agenda in two hours."

When someone is succinct and specific, a definite, observable event occurs. I see this en masse when I run workshops, and I find it so amusing I'm going to share my bird's-eye view with you. Imagine I am standing at the front of a training room with twenty executives. I ask someone named Analise what she likes about living in her home, requesting her to be specific. "It's comfortable," Analise responds, having gotten the succinct bit down easily.

If you looked around the training room at that moment you'd see the same look on everyone's face. They would be squinting slightly, trying to understand what Analise meant. Next I ask Analise to be more specific: whether she meant comfortable like an old shoe, or that it's worth a million dollars, or that she has so many maids she doesn't have to do anything.

After my explanation, Analise says: "Well, it's really comfortable—we have lots of oversized colorful cushions spread over big soft couches, and you feel like wearing comfy clothes all the time and lounging around." Now if you were standing in my place at the front of the room, instead of squinting, this time you'd see almost everyone nodding, right at the very same moment.

I have seen this hundreds of times now: When other people are able to make their own mental picture of what we're saying, their brain sends a signal to the head to nod a little. It's unconscious, and it's universal. So if you're paying attention when you communicate, it's easy to tell when you've been specific—just watch people's head movements.

Being specific takes a little effort, often more effort than we put into our conversations day to day. Being specific requires that we pay close attention to what other people say, to make an extra effort to mentally note the key points so we can be accurate and detailed in our responses. (Notice how much more specific I was in that last sentence, compared to simply saying, "You need to stop and think.")

Being specific builds trust between you and the person you are trying to develop. Being succinct *and* specific together means including everything that's relevant in a dialogue, and nothing irrelevant.

■ ■ ■ ■ ■ ■ ■ **EXERCISE STATION FOR** ■ ■ ■ ■ ■ ■ ■ ■

Be Specific

Practice being specific for a day. Focus your attention on providing the full story in every conversation, though just in summary so you are still being succinct. Write down what you notice.

_____

_____

_____

_____

_____

_____

BE GENEROUS

Be profound, be funny, or be quiet.

SOURCE UNKNOWN

Once we have focused on being succinct and specific, the final component of speaking with intent is to use words that will have the biggest positive impact on the other person. We want to be "generous" within our conversations.

To illustrate this, let's go back to the example of Saul, the production manager who'd worked late nights for a week. If you were Saul's boss and he'd confided in you about the difficulties he had getting his project done on time, a generous response might be: "I appreciate you being open about your challenges. I know it might have been a bit of a risk and I appreciate you letting me have a chance to help you here."

Put succinctly, being generous is about giving: of yourself.

Put succinctly and specifically, being generous is about speaking so that the other person relates to what you are saying, by using words they will connect with, and doing everything you can to ensure they fully understand where you are coming from.

Put succinctly, specifically, and generously, being generous is about being committed to the other person getting your message. It means putting yourself in their shoes when you're speaking, taking care to make sure every word you use is just right, and focusing on their needs in the conversation. It also means sharing a bit of your humanity.

Being generous is a subtle thing. I have found that people need to find their own words with this third part of Speak With Intent, more so than the other two parts. Here are some of the things to be aware of when being generous.

Choosing your words

Being generous is about using the best language possible in each conversation. It means slowing down a little so you have a chance to choose your words carefully, so that people understand exactly what you are trying to say.

Being sensitive

Being generous means caring enough to be sensitive to how you come across. Nothing you say should be jarring or off-putting. Instead of saying "I think you should stop focusing on that" you might say "I sense it might be worth giving that less focus." It's not about being cagey; it's about being a bit sensitive so something you say doesn't throw people off balance.

Paying attention

In this multitasking world, it's rare to give someone your undivided attention. Being generous means giving people all of your focus, rather than speaking to them while emailing or thinking about other issues—such as what you're going to say next.

Acknowledging people

Being generous is also about giving people lots of encouragement, validation, and acknowledgment. It doesn't have to be in a lot of words; it can simply be a matter of how you come across, of the little words of thanks you give. It's an attitude. If you want people to think big thoughts, you need them to feel safe.

Being human

Being generous is all about being personal, being real. It means sharing your humanity, being open about what's important to you. Sharing personal information can help people feel more at ease with you and therefore more willing to think challenging thoughts.

In summary, being generous is a way of showing you care about the other person. It helps build the level of trust required for doing the work of improving thinking. Being generous invites the other person to take the conversation to a deeper level, away from the surface facts and details, into vision and planning, into higher thoughts. Being generous opens up the possibility of learning and change.

BEING SUCCINCT, SPECIFIC, AND GENEROUS IN PRACTICE

When I ask participants during workshops what it will take for them to speak with intent, a funny thing often happens. Someone will begin to blurt something out, then stop themselves. After quietly reflecting for a moment, they'll speak slower and more thoughtfully than normal, then state a version of "I really don't know, it's something I have never had to do, it's going to take some focus and commitment." At this moment the rest of the group sees that this person has just exhibited exactly what it takes to speak with intent: to become quiet, reflective, and to speak the truth.

Speak with Intent is not a model you can integrate logically by trying to keep each piece in mind at once. The elements of this model are more like general signposts, not specific paths to follow. As everyone is different, you may need to find your own way to integrate these ideas. I personally find that to speak with intent I need to take a moment to reflect, to check in with myself, and pay attention to what I am feeling and sensing. Then I need to give myself the time to speak at a pace that allows me to actually be honest with myself. There— how was that for succinct, specific and generous?

I am not suggesting that everyone in the workplace speaks with this much intent the whole time. Step three is about learning a new way to communicate when you are taking on the challenge of improving performance. These conversations are just like flying down a steep highway on a bicycle: It's good to slow your thoughts right down and focus on the moment, so that you don't end up causing yourself or others any pain.

Quiet Leaders speak with intent. They are succinct, specific, and generous a lot of the time, especially when they are trying to transform performance. Speaking this way provides a foundation for real change to occur.

■ ■ ■ ■ ■ ■ ■ **EXERCISE STATION FOR** ■ ■ ■ ■ ■ ■ ■

Speak with Intent

This is one of the more challenging assignments in the book, as we're talking about speaking differently, and speaking is something that's deeply hardwired. However, if you remember the chapters on how the brain works, the key is not to try and undo what we do, but to do something different.

My suggestion is to reread this step including all three elements every day, to remind yourself of the principles. Find opportunities to become aware of how you are speaking. Reflect more before speaking. Take the time to consider your words before blurting.

You might like to try this on people close to you, and tell them what you are doing so that you can get feedback from them.

A WORD ON DIGITAL COMMUNICATIONS

The ideas within Speak With Intent are extremely relevant when it comes to using our most common form of business communication: email. The amount of anxiety that email is generating in organizations is something we need to take more seriously. Many workers claim this is the most stressful part of their job. Let's explore how the ideas covered in this chapter might help here.

Nearly everyone I ask about this issue complains that they are drowning in emails. I hear statements like "It's driving me crazy," "I can't cope," and "I feel I'm losing my mind." I expect that this issue alone is driving many otherwise talented people to opt out of corporate life.

Given that our brains change in response to inputs from the world, the incredible volume of information we now deal with, driven by email communications, is pushing our brain to make connections at a pace never seen before. To put this in perspective, consider that the average seventeenth-century Frenchman had as much information stored in mind in their lifetime as is contained every Sunday in the *New York Times*. The outside world has changed a lot since then, but our brains may not yet have had enough time to catch up. Even ten years ago people didn't have to try and respond intelligently to forty different complex issues in thirty minutes, as we often do first thing each morning after downloading email.

Anything that reduces the quantity of emails is a positive thing. Anything that makes an email as clear as humanly possible is great too. Try using as few words as you can so that when people scan through your email, which is one out of a hundred, they can comprehend what you are saying at a glance. Perhaps even go back over emails before you send them. If it's a long complex email, leave it in your outbox and come back with the clarity of distance a few hours later.

A rule I try to keep is if an email takes up more than one screen then I don't send it. Instead I email an agenda and schedule a time to have a phone call. This can save an immense amount of time and energy, firstly because people simply don't read long emails, and secondly if they do, a response to a long email is often just as long and tends to be not very productive. With the cost of telecommunications plummeting, in some cases to one cent a minute or less, there's no excuse not to pick up the phone now.

Bill Gates, in *Business @ the Speed of Thought,* said that he always signed off emails with a smile, as there were too many other emotions flying around the Internet. And this brings up a big issue. I have yet to meet someone in the modern world who has not lost several days of productivity because of an upsetting email. And it's not as though people get a little annoyed. They get really angry, then spend hours writing an email back, then they get another back in return that's even more nasty in its tone, and on it goes. The technical term for this is "flaming" and it's nasty business. It saps the energy of both parties, of the people around them, and it's often completely avoidable and unnecessary. If the same people had covered the issues by telephone, the emotional impact would probably have been far less.

I've developed a set of guidelines for email that I find I can stick to almost the whole time, and I ask my staff to follow them as well. The basic principle is that emails are only to be used to share data and information, and to schedule live conversations. It means that we don't email anything of a remotely personal nature—unless it's 100 percent pure positive feedback. Anything that might bring about an emotional response for either the sender or the receiver doesn't get sent. I am talking about anything personal, any type of feedback. It's like an imaginary filter we put on all emails. Sometimes it's helpful to write the email, to get it off your chest, but then save it in a drafts folder and delete it a week later.

Over the years I have watched new team members apply this principle, and it sometimes takes time to create these new habits. We think that by emailing we won't have to deal with emotionally charged issues, when in fact the opposite is the case. We now have a firm rule about this—it's company policy—and no one is willing to hear people's stories if they break the rule. It's a fantastic discipline that saves significant person-hours each year.

In a big organization, putting this one guideline in place might save millions of dollars a year. As well as reducing conflicts, it also means that the right type of conversational medium is being used to tackle complex issues. This reduces those annoying emails that can end up bouncing between people for weeks. It also means that ideas are shared better, that people understand each other more often, and that people collaborate more efficiently. It's an attention economy not just in the brain but in organizations as well—we need to maximize the use of everyone's attention. Applying guidelines like these to the use of email results in the more efficient use of attention, and time all around.

Here's my full list of guidelines for how to apply the principles of this chapter to email communication.

1. Emails should contain as few words as possible.
2. Make it easy to see your central point at a glance, in one screen.
3. Never send an email that could emotionally affect another person unless it's pure positive feedback.
4. Emotional issues must be discussed by phone; email should be used only to book a time for a call.
5. If you accidentally break rule number four, phone the person immediately, apologize, and discuss the issue by phone.

DANCE TOWARD INSIGHT

To learn is to change how you think.

MICHAEL MERZENICH (1992)

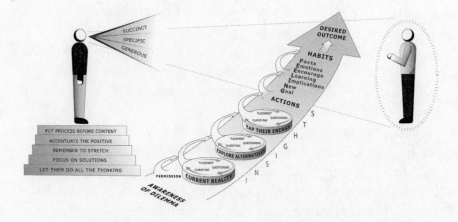

Figure 20, The Six Steps to Transforming Performance

Step four, Dance Toward Insight, is the central step in this book. In this step we explore a whole new way of having conversations with people, a process map for conversations when our impact is equal to or exceeds our intent.

Much of this step is about creating an environment in which people have insights for themselves. We work through a series of elements that will help you follow the shortest path from A to B that I mentioned earlier in the book. These elements, permission, place-ment, questioning and clarifying, weave together into this new process for having dialogues that help people think better, without telling anyone what to do, in a way that truly transforms perfor-mance. Before we get into this in detail, I want to introduce a little more science here.

Imagine you are standing at a street corner in a strange city. You're about to meet a friend for dinner at a specific restaurant, but there are no taxis around, so you have to walk. You're standing on this corner holding two different maps of the same area, but these maps each give you different directions for how to get to the restaurant: one says go left, the other go right. What do you do?

Like most people you'd pore over the maps for a while, trying to decide which set of instructions was right. You'd probably feel stuck in the one place and somewhat frustrated. Eventually you might ask for assistance from someone. When this person asks if you've checked the dates of the maps, you have a big "aha" and see the thing you hadn't noticed: one map is older than the other, and the restau-rant must have moved in the interim. Suddenly it feels like a weight has lifted off you, and away you go.

When we have not been able to think our way through a situation, we are just like the person standing on the street corner: we're miss-ing a key insight that will help us move toward our goal. Quiet Lead-ers are the persons you go to for help. Quiet Leaders are catalysts for insights: people have more insights when they are around. How-ever, the way they do this is quite unusual. Quiet Leaders won't tell you where the restaurant is, or tell you one map is older than the other. They know there's tremendous power and motivation in other people coming to their own insights. So they take another ap-proach.

Before we dive into this other approach, let's explore the last major piece of science I will introduce about the nature of insights themselves.

THE FOUR FACES OF INSIGHT

To connect known concepts in new ways—this is the nature of many insights, the recognition of new connections across existing knowledge.

MARC JUNG-BEEMAN ET AL (2004)

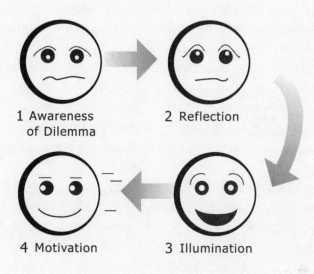

Figure 19, The Four Faces of Insight

Awareness of dilemma

In early 2005, after several years of talking about neuroscience in workshops, I got excited about finding out what was going on in the brain when people were having insights using the models I had developed. I secured a small grant to run an fMRI (functional magnetic resonance imaging) study of what was going on in the brain during coaching. I then gathered a team of volunteers who had completed my training program.[25] We called the project "The anatomy of an 'Aha!' "

The team was led by Marisa Galisteo, a former research scientist from the NYU medical center who had crossed over from cancer research to executive coaching. She had made the change in order to make more of a difference to the world, but had not left her passion for science behind when she changed careers. Over several months of meetings and conversations, and having read a ton of literature on what was known about insights, we developed a good body of knowledge on the field. We also discovered that a lot of research had already been done in very similar territory, such as an fMRI study of insight[26] by Marc Jung-Beeman, John Kounios, and others, published in April 2004, and several other relevant studies.[27] These studies were all fascinating, and breaking new ground, but there was nothing that tied all the findings together in a relevant, accessible way.

During a long flight, while reading over a series of papers, I had a sudden energizing flash. In an instant I pictured how people's faces changed considerably when they had an insight. I felt strongly that if leaders could recognize which "face" people had on at any time, it might make them more effective at improving thinking. So we set about trying to coalesce the existing knowledge into a simple model that defined what happened in the few seconds before, during, and after someone had an insight.[28]

What's exciting about this model is we now have visual and audible clues to watch for when we're trying to help other people have their own insights, which makes the whole process more tangible. Let's take a look at each face in more detail.

The first part of having an insight is the identification of some kind of problem to be solved. When we first become aware of a dilemma, our face looks a little unhappy, perplexed. Our eyes might be squinting slightly, we recognize we have a problem, we feel stuck. In the restaurant example, we've realized we don't know the way, so we've stopped in our tracks. We haven't yet thought hard enough about the problem, but we definitely know there is an issue to resolve here.

In the workplace, the majority of development conversations between leaders and their employees involve ideas that someone has not yet been able to reconcile, like the person looking for the restaurant at the start of this step. Some examples of workplace dilemmas include:

> "I want to know how to inspire my sales people but they don't seem to care."
> "I'd really like to get all my projects finished but am overloaded with emails."
> "I don't want to let my boss down but need some down time."
> "I don't like that new salesperson, and I'm not sure how I can work with them."

People express their dilemmas in more complex terms than this at first, but it's been my experience that at the core of any complex conversation is a two-part dilemma waiting to be clarified. We will come back to how we do that a bit later on. For now I want to make this point: The conversations leaders have with their employees that will make the most substantial difference to their performance, involve resolving a dilemma. The most effective way to resolve their dilemma is to help the other person have an insight for themselves. The first step toward this is to identify the dilemma itself.

From a neuroscientific perspective, a dilemma means we have various mental maps in conflict. They have competing values, competing demands for resources, and the brain has not yet worked out how to resolve this conflict by creating a new metamap or by reconfiguring our existing maps. For example, we might want to be more successful, but think this means we need to work longer hours—yet we also want to focus on our health and fitness. Our brain can't yet see how to reconcile the needs of these different desires. And while we know there is an impasse, we haven't given the problem enough thought or the right attention yet to come up with a useful answer.

Reflection

You can clearly tell when someone is reflecting on an issue: his or her face changes. Most people look up, or slightly up and across, and get a dazed look on their face. Their mouth might tense up as they think more deeply. Nearly everyone becomes very silent for a moment. We all know this feeling. Going back to the restaurant example, we've stopped walking and we're looking up at the sky, reflecting on what we should do, but not getting any answers yet.

Jung-Beeman et al[29] reported that when people did come up with an insight, their brains were giving off alpha-band waves just beforehand. Alpha waves correlate with people shutting down inputs from their external senses and focusing on internal stimuli. It's been shown that top athletes' brains give off alpha waves just before an excellent performance.[30] Alpha waves have also been found to correlate with the release of the neurotransmitter serotonin, a chemical messenger that increases relaxation and eases pain.[31] So when we reflect, we also tend to feel good.

However, alpha waves are also decreased by doing math calculations[32] and other exercises that require engaging the conscious, logical mind. I propose that there is a certain type of internal reflection that brings about insights, that we don't make these big connections through deductive reasoning or pure calculation.[33] Our ten-cent computer may not cut it.

Studies have shown that during reflection we are not thinking logically or analyzing data; we're using a part of our brain used for making links across the whole brain.[34] We are thinking in an unusual way, allowing our unconscious brain to work. We're tapping into more intelligence than the seven pieces of information we can hold at once in our working memory.

In practical terms, it seems that to help people have insights, we need to encourage them to reflect more, and think less—or at least less logically.

Illumination

The illumination phase is the most thoroughly studied part of the process, and something we're all familiar with. Being in the illumination phase brings on a rush of energy. If it's a big idea, like the scientific challenge that Archimedes solved while in the bath,[35] we might run through the streets naked as he did. Or at least do the modern equivalent: send ten emails.

Even small illuminations pack an energetic punch. Think for a moment about the buzz you get watching a whodunit police show or a great movie, when right at the end the mystery all falls into place. This rush is being driven by nothing more than a new set of connections in our brain. And we get this same rush when we solve a dilemma at work for ourselves, too.

Right at the moment of insight neurotransmitters, such as adrenaline,[36] are released, giving us that well-known rush. Other neurotransmitters, such as dopamine and serotonin, are possibly given off as well. Having an insight is one of life's most pleasant moments.

According to the Jung-Beeman paper,[37] at the very moment an insight occurs, the brain gives off strong gamma-band waves. Gamma-band waves are the only frequency found in all parts of the brain, and are seen when the brain simultaneously processes information across different regions.[38] As Roger Traub, when professor of mathematical neuroscience at the University of Birmingham (U.K.), said, "Gamma rhythms appear to be involved in higher mental activity, including perception and consciousness. It seems to be associated with consciousness, e.g. it disappears with general anaesthesia. A lack of gamma waves signifies learning difficulties in people."

Gamma-band brain waves signify various parts of the brain forming a new map. Or as neuroscientist John Ratey says: "The different pieces of the concept are transported back and forth between the regions that house them, until they resonate with each other—sustained at the 40 Hz oscillation . . ."[39]

When we have an illumination experience we are creating a supermap (of other maps) that links many parts of the brain. The creation of this new map gives off substantial energy, energy that can be tapped as a valuable resource. Imagine 1,000 employees having insights once a day, instead of once a year: I wonder what that would do to the levels of engagement in any workplace.

Motivation

When people are in the motivation phase, their eyes are racing ahead, ready to take action. They've already jumped out of their seat and are off doing something, hence the eyes going to the left in the picture of this model.

However, the intense motivation we feel passes quickly. An hour after a great idea we have just about forgotten it. You might know this feeling: You've just had a big insight about how to reorganize a project and you're feeling excited by some new ideas. But if you are fairly self-aware, you also know that your motivation to do something will pass fairly quickly. You don't necessarily have to fix everything right away, but if you don't write down a few ideas while the concept is fresh in your mind, there is a chance you might lose the idea.

If you can get people to take tangible actions while the illumination is close at hand, even just to commit to doing something later, this will be a big help in ensuring new ideas become reality.

The Four Faces of Insight is a guide to the anatomy of the aha. It is useful in several ways. For example, if you're talking to someone and their eyes go up, the best thing might be to say nothing for a moment. And when people have an insight, it's important to get them to act on their ideas quickly, as the energy for action fades fast. With this understanding of what happens when we have an aha, next we'll explore a set of conversation tools for bringing about real insights in others.

■ ■ ■ ■ ■ ■ ■ **EXERCISE STATION FOR** ■ ■ ■ ■ ■ ■ ■

The Four Faces of Insight

Explain the Four Faces of Insight to someone you speak to a lot. Then see if you notice the different faces during your conversations. This can be quite a fun and eye-opening exercise. Make some notes about what you notice.

_____

_____

_____

_____

_____

THE DANCE OF INSIGHT

The principal activities of brains are making changes in themselves.

MARVIN L. MINSKY (1986)

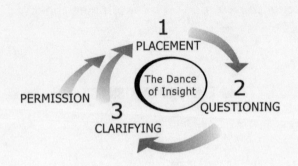

Figure 21, The Dance of Insight

The Four Faces of Insight model describes what happens when someone has an aha. The Dance of Insight model tells you how to actually make these ahas happen.

The Dance of Insight is a way of keeping people fully engaged with you in the delicate dance of making new connections. This model helps people develop a deeper awareness of their dilemma, puts them into a reflective phase, then encourages those aha moments to come through.

Let me give this model more context. While teaching my coaching skills workshops, I noticed several common traps people fell into. These were:

1. Rushing the other person: either getting too personal too quickly, without making sure this was okay, or not giving the other person the space to engage their brain.
2. Thinking harder about the issue than the person with the issue: if anyone was having insights, it was the coach!

3. Both parties getting lost: people were asking question after question, the result being the conversation went on a lot of tangents. I kept hearing people say "What were we talking about again?"

With these traps in mind I built a way to improve the *process* of having insight conversations, whatever the *content* was. While I initially created the Dance of Insight for coaching dialogues, this model has proven to be very useful any time we want another person to engage more deeply in a thinking process and come up with insights for themselves. So it's now being applied by thousands of leaders, facilitators, trainers, consultants, teachers, and even counselors, in many different settings.

When the Dance of Insight model is delivered well, the leader becomes almost invisible in the conversation. It's like the way a facilitator at a corporate retreat makes sure the day has a solid structure to it: they ensure the goals for the retreat are clear, that everyone is engaged, and that the conversation stays on track. But the facilitator doesn't do the thinking; that's up to the team. When we use the Dance of Insight model, we are helping the other person stay on track, but we're also staying out of the way—we're their "invisible dance partner."

The Dance of Insight is in four parts. It starts with the concept of establishing permission, then there are three elements that go in a circular pattern: placement, questioning, and clarifying. I've found it's helpful to deconstruct the model first and learn each step on its own, and then reconstruct it in your own language once you know the parts.

Finally, while the elements of permission, placement, questioning, and clarifying are central to resolving dilemmas, each element can be useful in many other applications as well. Let's explore each element from both perspectives now.

PERMISSION

Respect a man, he will do the more.

JAMES HOWELL (1594–1666)

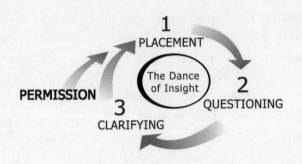

Figure 22, The Dance of Insight

Have you ever had the joy of trying to dance with someone who didn't want to dance with you? If so, perhaps you noticed that no amount of enthusiasm on your part could make up for a lack of willingness on theirs. (Yes, I did learn this the hard way in my youth.) It's the same with conversations when we want people to think more deeply than usual: we need their explicit permission to get personal; otherwise we could be fighting a losing battle.

When I first identified this concept of establishing permission in a dialogue, I began to notice that I was having a lot of conversations across the board that I didn't really have "permission" to have. I seemed to just barge in and start talking anyway, ignoring people's signals. Speaking to people at times felt like a bit of a battle. Recognizing this was a little unnerving at first.

I started to apply the concept of establishing permission in the executive coaching I was doing and it had a dramatic impact on my sessions. By checking for permission before getting any more personal with people, I noticed I was getting less resistance to having harder conversations, and we spent less time on sidetracks. I then started to apply this concept to conversations with my team. I began to ask people if they'd be willing to talk about an issue, before launching into the conversation. I found this made harder conversations, like reviewing someone's sales for the week, a lot easier.

Since then I've made establishing permission an unconscious habit—I do it at the beginning of most phone calls, meetings, or conversations. Over years of using this principle, teaching it, and writing about it, I uncovered several insights about permission that you might find helpful.

Permission comes in levels

The territories we are comfortable talking about vary with different people we talk to. If I haven't met you before, I don't have permission to walk into your bathroom and ask why you use a certain brand of toothpaste. If I am your best friend, I do. As your partner I can ask for your bank balance, something even a best friend can't. It's interesting to note that we come back to the place where we leave off: if two best friends don't see each other for years, the levels of permission are likely to remain intact.

We're very attuned to permission

Most people can comfortably name ten colleagues and describe the conversations they could strike up without needing to establish permission. My guess is there are evolutionary advantages to knowing how to interact with other people in a way that ensures social harmony. While one person could be comfortable explaining their chest infection to a stranger, another person could find this highly inappropriate. To Europeans it's fine to touch people on the shoulder, it's a sign of friendliness. To Americans this is more rare, by a factor of around ten to one.[40] So there are cultural and social issues involved in levels of permission, as well as individual differences.

Remember that we have a strong tendency to think everyone's brain is just like ours, so we assume others have the same boundaries we do. This may not be correct at all, and once we get too personal too quickly, there's no going back.

Put all the reasons above together and you have a strong case for always asking before getting more personal with anyone. And there's almost nothing more personal than trying to change people's thinking. Given that our perceptions are reality, asking people to think differently means we're tinkering with their very existence.

Let's explore all the different situations where you might use this concept of establishing permission before having a dialogue.

Starting a new conversation

People at work are busy. Try establishing permission any time you want someone to stop what he or she is doing and speak with you about an issue that will require them to think differently. This is a simple way of showing that you respect someone's mental space, and creates a lot of trust. With a colleague at work you could say "I'd like to talk to you about that new project—is now a good time?" Asking permission might result in scheduling a better time to speak, which is much better than launching into a conversation that someone isn't willing to have.

Any time you get more personal in a conversation

I mentioned that permission has different levels. There are quite obvious boundaries between each level, like floors in an office building. You might start off on the ground floor talking about the weather with someone. If you want to ask them about a work project you need to subtly check to see if this is okay, which is going to the first floor. Then to ask a more personal question, such as how they are feeling about their job at the moment, that would be going up a floor, so you'd check again. Asking about their health is up a floor again. Anytime you move up a level, ask permission, or people can become defensive. Then they stop listening to you and start listening to their internal dialogue. More to the point, if you *do* ask permission enough, people will feel safe, acknowledged, and respected.

How to establish permission for a conversation

I rarely use the word "permission" when establishing permission; the word itself sounds a little odd. You will find your own words for this concept that suit your natural conversational style. Here are some examples of words you might use to establish permission:

> "I get a sense you have more to say about that, could I probe a little further?"
>
> "I'd like to have a more open conversation than we've had before, would it be okay if I asked you some more specific questions right now?"
>
> "Can we spend a few minutes brainstorming ideas around this?"
>
> "I'd like to understand more about your thinking in that area, would you be okay talking more about that?"
>
> "I'd like to discuss some more personal matters . . . would that be okay with you?"

I've had a few managers say that since they are the boss, they don't ever need to ask permission to ask their team a question. They're right—they don't *need* to. However, when you have a position of power and establish permission anyway, it can have a big positive impact on work relationships. It builds trust, and because people feel safer around you they are likely to open up more.

Let's bring the concept of permission alive with a dialogue involving Sally and Paul from the bank, whom I introduced earlier in the book. Sally wants to talk to Paul about a project that's not going well. She knows the issue is emotionally charged, but wants to broach it with Paul anyway, since she feels he needs to give the project more focus. (At least she thinks that's what Paul needs to do, as we will see a bit later.) Without the concept of permission, the conversation might go like this.

Sally: *Paul, I'm getting a bit concerned about that project.*
Paul: *It's okay, don't worry about it, it'll be fine. No need to be concerned.*

In this instance Paul picks up on Sally's tone and gets slightly defensive. The conversation Sally wanted to have doesn't happen, and there is also a subtle break in trust.

Or it might be worse, and go like this instead:

Sally: *Paul, I'm getting a bit concerned about that project.*
Paul: *I've done everything I can, give me a break and get off my case, will you?*

As well as being defensive, Paul's now getting annoyed. Sally might then react to his response, resulting in a bigger breakdown in trust between them. Not only has Sally not been able to manage Paul's performance—worse than that, she has slightly damaged their relationship by trying.

This kind of interaction happens all the time in the workplace. After an interaction like this, a lot of managers decide it's best not to give people any feedback at all: better to stay out of the way and at least do no harm. I believe this is one of the reasons "Not getting quality feedback" and "Not knowing what's expected of me" are two of the biggest complaints workers have. Interacting about people's performance can go wrong very quickly, especially with smart, independent thinkers.

Here's how Sally might use the concept of permission in this situation:

Sally: *Paul, I'd like to have a conversation about something that's a bit delicate to talk about. It might take us fifteen minutes or so—is this a good place and now a good time? It's about that project that I know is on both of our minds a lot.*
Paul: *Ahhh . . . I was focusing on this other thing right now, but okay, can we do this later?*
Sally: *Sure, thanks. What about three o'clock today over coffee downstairs?*

Instead of launching into a dialogue without warning, Sally has set up an opportunity to get Paul's full attention, and therefore there's more chance he's going to be open during the conversation. There is much greater chance that Sally's impact will be the same as her intent this time.

Now you might think this is pretty basic. It is. However, take a look at what's happening around you at work. Do people ask your permission before launching into big conversations, checking it's an okay time for you? Do they respect the state of your brain before throwing a new topic at you? Even though this concept is basic, people just aren't doing it.

Asking permission significantly increases our chance of having a great dance with someone, a dance involving a high-level conversation that improves people's thinking. Don't look like I used to on the dance floor sometimes, flailing about over-enthusiastically, trying to get the other person to smile. Ask first. If they say no, try again later.

■ ■ ■ ■ ■ ■ ■ EXERCISE STATION FOR ■ ■ ■ ■ ■ ■ ■

Permission

Practice asking permission every time you sense that either you or the other person has an emotional charge around a topic. A useful proving ground to grow new mental muscles here could be with your kids. Try asking permission to have a difficult conversation before actually having it: many parents have found this to be a home-changing experience! And if the kids say no to the dialogue, you need to respect this, otherwise you might do more harm than good. However, don't forget you can always ask them to make a time, or ask if you can ask again at another time.

If you don't have kids to practice on, try asking permission at work once a day. Get in the habit of asking to have any new conversation, anything that will require someone to mentally shift gears. Using this skill often will help you naturally start to ask for permission when you want to get more personal. Make some notes below about what you notice from starting to ask permission.

_____

_____

_____

_____

_____

PLACEMENT

*Placement is your friend. When you get lost in the forest
of a conversation, go back to the last time you knew
your location and place yourself there.*

DAVID ROCK (2003)

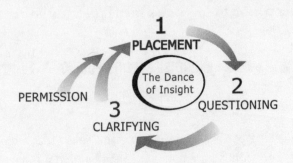

Figure 23, The Dance of Insight

We're still in the fourth step to transforming performance, which is
to Dance Toward Insight. So far we've explored the concept of what
happens when we have an aha, with the Four Faces of Insight model.
Then I introduced the concept of the Dance of Insight, a model
made up of four elements, which is about how to generate these ahas.
We've just covered the first part of the Dance of Insight, permission,
a useful tool for starting off any difficult conversation. Once we have
people's permission to get a little more personal, the next step is
something I call placement. Placement is about anchoring any conversation: defining exactly where you are and what's about to happen
next, so that the people are thinking about exactly the same issues
from similar perspectives.

Take another look at the whole last paragraph: it was an example
of pure placement, letting you know where we've been, where we are,
and where we're going. Whenever I start a new conversation, or take
an existing conversation to a new level, or start a new chapter, I find

using placement helps both me and the other person know where we are. It helps place us in the conversation, hence the name.

In the workplace I find that two colleagues often have different conversations while talking to one another. One person might talk about the need for goals while the other talks about budgets being slashed. There's nothing dramatically wrong with this, except when you want to have quite a complex or difficult conversation, such as interacting with a staff member about their performance. Here we need to be very explicit about what's being discussed, otherwise the conversation could go in circles—or worse, end up in a heap. Overall I find that the more subtle or emotionally charged a conversation is, the easier it is to get lost in the details or problems, and the more that placement helps the conversation stay on track and be useful.

Here's an example of how you might place a team member before doing a biannual performance review:

Before we start with the review let me tell you a bit about what's going to happen. First, I want you to know that I am committed to this conversation being useful for you, and if it starts feeling like it's not useful I'll stop and check in with both of us and see what we need to change. Second, I am here in the role of your reviewer, not as your manager, so I am not going to get too detailed. I want to stay at a high level with the process. Third, I want you to have a chance to give yourself lots of feedback before I give you any. And finally, we're going to take an hour to answer the questions together, and you can add any other items to the conversation that you'd like. Is that all good with you?

Can you see how we take care of the other person with placement? Many people naturally use placement before an unusually difficult conversation. I find it can make a big difference in the vast majority of dialogues we have at work, not just the tough ones.

When you place people in a conversation, you take care of issues like:

- Setting the scene
- How long you'd like to speak for
- Where you're coming from
- What your goal for the conversation is
- What you would like them to do in the conversation
- How you would like them to listen
- What's going to happen in the conversation
- What you're looking to achieve from the dialogue

Placement takes care of the "why, when, how, and who" of the conversation. When you place someone well, the conversation unfolds better than when you don't. Placement keeps the other person with you in the conversation and beside you on the journey. It sets up the possibility of dancing in time together, instead of one of you dancing and the other person being dragged across the room.

There are many instances you can use placement: at the start of a meeting, in a difficult conversation with someone, or when you're short on time and have a lot to discuss. Placement is a helpful resource any time you have a conversation you'd like to go well.

Let's go back to the example with Sally and Paul:

Sally: *Paul, I'd like to have a conversation about something that's a bit delicate to talk about. It might take us fifteen minutes or so—is this a good place and time for you? It's about the new sales project.*

Paul: *Ahhh . . . I was focusing on this other thing right now, but okay, let's chat. Do you want to sit down?*

Sally: *Thanks a lot for making the time. I want to chat about the project but I also know you're putting a lot of work into it, and are really focused on it right now. I am not here to tell you you're doing anything wrong. I am keen to keep track of how it's going, and want to see how you are feeling about the project to see if there is a way I could be of any help, to be a sounding board at all. Would that be okay?*

Now how could anyone react badly to that? Sally has made it explicit that she's there to help, that she's not going to give him a hard time. His guard is now down. If there is any defensiveness it will be a lot less than without the placement. Notice a little permission crept into the end of her placement, something that often gets added into the mix when you use these models.

When you have placed people effectively in a conversation, they are clear about what's going to happen. You can then move more smoothly to the next step in the Dance of Insight, asking questions.

Placing people repeatedly

It's logical to use placement when starting a new conversation. However, if you only placed people at the start you would be missing half the value of this tool. Difficult conversations have a habit of going all over the place and getting off point. Placement is something you can use every minute or so, sometimes even more, to guide a complex conversation and keep it on track. When we use placement we are not just placing the other person, we are also placing ourselves in the purpose of the dialogue, we are anchoring our own thoughts in the direction we want to go.

In this instance placement becomes a summary of the points you have covered so far in a dialogue, to remind you both about where you are, and identify the best path to follow next. Placement is a discipline which, once you learn it, can dramatically impact how quickly a conversation achieves its intent.

To illustrate this, let's see how Peter, a senior executive at a large consulting company, might debrief with his head of learning, Michelle, about a training she attended. Peter wants Michelle to be explicit about what she got out of the training, to know if it was worth the hefty investment. Peter could use placement up front and then continually as in the example below.

Peter: *Can you chat for a few minutes now?* [Asking permission.]
Michelle: *Sure.*

Peter: *I'd like to have an in-depth conversation with you to get a handle on what you got out of that workshop, so that I can understand what the value was, and help you integrate the learning. I'd like to get a little detailed, would now be a good time for you?*

Michelle: *Okay, let me just put these papers aside so I can focus.*

Peter: *Thanks.* [Small appreciations are useful for making people feel safe.]

Peter: *I am interested specifically in what you learned, and then how you think you might apply your insights to your role as the head of the learning team.* [Being succinct and specific.] *I know some of the issues in the course could have been personal so I want you to know you don't have to tell me everything.* [Being generous.] *Maybe we should just focus on the high points, what do you think?* [Checking in that she is placed and everything is clear.]

Next Peter would ask a thinking question, which we will get to in the next chapter, then after Michelle spoke, Peter would stop and summarize what was said. He might say:

Peter: *So let's see if I'm on track with you . . . you liked the workshop and had some insights about how to be more effective, and how to run your weekly meetings with more focus, and how to organize your schedule a bit better.* [Good placement summarizing where the dialogue is up to, which focused both people onto the intent of the conversation too.]

As you'll see when we put this all together at the end of step four, placement is an extremely useful tool that can make your job as a leader a whole lot easier. Placement may be one of your best tools for staying on track with the goal of transforming performance and avoiding a lot of unnecessary conversations lost in details, problems, or worse, drama.

■ ■ ■ ■ ■ ■ ■ **EXERCISE STATION FOR** ■ ■ ■ ■ ■ ■ ■ ■

Placement

Practice placing people once a day. You could try it at the start of a meeting, talking about timing, roles, outcomes, and process, and see what happens. My experience is a little placement goes a long way to making just about every dialogue significantly more efficient.

_____

_____

_____

_____

_____

_____

_____

QUESTIONING

The uncreative mind can spot wrong answers, but it takes a very creative mind to spot wrong questions.

ANTHONY JAY

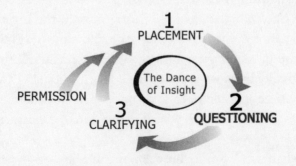

Figure 24, The Dance of Insight

Once we have established permission to have a difficult conversation, and have used placement to outline where we are coming from, we're now in a strong position to start helping someone think more deeply. If we want the other person to be doing all the thinking, asking questions is the only way forward.

Learning to ask powerful questions is the most central skill in this book. When we ask the right questions, people move into phase two of the Faces of Insight: they reflect and their brains go into the alpha state. If we ask enough of the right questions, people often have their own aha.

The question, of course, now is, what is the right type of questions to ask? To answer this question I'd like to bring back a concept I brought up at the introduction to the Six Steps: the concept of the dilemma. Then I will ask *you* a few questions to see if you can come to an answer yourself about which types of questions are best to ask to transform performance. If you don't want to do that, feel free to jump to page 129.

Imagine you're chatting with a colleague over a drink one evening. Let's call her Yvonne. While talking about your respective jobs, Yvonne says: "I'd really like to be less stressed at work, but it just seems to get busier every week." Yvonne's statement is an example of an everyday dilemma. She has an issue she's been trying to resolve, but as yet there's no solution.

We all have lots of different dilemmas we're working on at any time. They are those thoughts that keep going around and around in our heads until they are resolved, like songs that repeat on the radio. We have our own Top Ten each month, the big issues we're working on, many of which aren't on the charts the next month. Then of course we have our version of the greatest hits of all time, the big unresolved dilemmas we seem to have heard forever. (I can't tell you how many times people have said to me "I'm stuck between a Rock and a hard place" when they're in some kind of dilemma that involves me.)

Going back to Yvonne, how could you help her have an insight here? What type of questions could you ask to help her resolve this dilemma?

■ ■ ■ ■ ■ ■ ■ **EXERCISE STATION FOR** ■ ■ ■ ■ ■ ■ ■
Questioning

Write down some questions you would ask Yvonne, so you can compare your approach to the ideas I am about to put forward.

_____

_____

_____

_____

We'll get back to what you wrote in a moment. First, I'd like to tell
you how I came up with my ideas about questioning. Over several
years I had the privilege of watching hundreds of professionals interact with other people's dilemmas as they participated in exercises in
my workshops. Over time I saw a defined set of common approaches
people used when they tried to question others. These include giving
advice in question form, focusing on the problems, focusing on the
details, rushing into action, and telling people how to think. As I illustrate each of our default modes for questioning next, take a look at
what you wrote down in this last exercise and see if you can distinguish your own default approach here.

While these approaches to questioning sometimes resulted in
useful conversations, they were definitely not taking the shortest distance from A to B. Over years of analyzing these interactions, I discovered there was another way of asking questions that was much
more effective than all the others, and it was a way that few people
naturally used. I will outline this best approach after going through
the other approaches.

Giving advice

A Quiet Leader gives less advice than almost anyone else on the planet.

The most common response to Yvonne's dilemma is to give
some kind of advice, phrased as a question. "Why don't you talk

to your boss?" we say, or, "What about taking up meditation or yoga?"

Unfortunately, our most common approach is also the one that's least likely to help, for several reasons. First, our chances of having an idea that's truly useful to Yvonne are slim. We learned about this in the section on the brain. We think we know what Yvonne needs, but in fact all we can see when we process Yvonne's dilemma is what *we* would need. Our advice is drawn from our own experiences, which are very different to other people's.

The second reason advice is rarely helpful is that people are far more likely to act on ideas they've come up with themselves, whereas other people's ideas tend to be automatically ignored or argued against. This is especially the case with intelligent, independent thinkers, the people who make up our corporate ranks today. I propose that if you have the exact idea that someone needs to hear, definitely don't tell them. If you do, you could be doing them a disservice.

The third reason advice is rarely useful is that the dilemma people first put forward is almost always *not* their main issue, once you drill down a little. This goes back to the very nature of dilemmas: If people were clear about the central challenge inside their dilemma, they probably would have solved the dilemma already.

For example, it might sound as though Yvonne's problem here is time management, so you go ahead and suggest she tackle her important tasks when she gets to work every morning. Yet when you help her think, Yvonne starts to make connections she had not yet made herself. Somehow the answer to Yvonne's dilemma is that she needs to purchase new drapes for her bedroom so she can sleep better—or something equally as unexpected. My experience is the answer to people's dilemmas is almost never related directly to what is first put forward as the central problem. Thus, until we help people make more connections, our advice will be off the mark most of the time.

Quiet Leaders give less advice than almost anyone else on the planet. That doesn't mean they can't share ideas or make suggestions—they do that a lot—but not necessarily right from the get-go. (We'll come back to this in step five, CREATE New Thinking.)

There are big upsides to not having to have the answers all the time: you can't be blamed for giving wrong advice; you don't have to think as hard; and most important, over time people will stop coming to you for answers and learn to think better for themselves.

Asking questions about the problem

Quiet Leaders, while they respect that people have problems, aren't all that interested in discussing them.

"It's obvious that asking Yvonne a broader question instead of giving her specific advice is going to work better," you may be saying to yourself. Certainly "ask, don't tell" is a common catch phrase in many management development programs. A broad question will tend to be more useful than giving advice; however, for some reason we all seem to go straight to asking questions about the problem. Questions like "Why do you think work's so stressful at the moment?" or "What are some of the big problems?" While these types of questions may result in an *interesting* conversation, most of the time this approach is not all that *useful*.

By being asked about how stressed she is, or any type of problem-focused question, Yvonne brings to mind her stresses and problems. She is now paying attention to these things. She might then talk about deadlines concerning her, go on to tell you about an argument with a colleague, and complain about her computer not working. She's now found three good reasons for why she's stressed. Has this reduced her stress? Remember that it's an attention economy in the brain: where we put our focus determines the wiring that we create.[41]

Asking about the source of the problem in a dialogue will probably result in someone having a good vent at you. Yvonne might feel that someone cares, and thus feel a little better, but her dilemma is rarely resolved in this instance.

It's a slippery slope to the problem. If you even get close to the edge you can find yourself sliding into reasons, justifications, and details.

Quiet Leaders, while they respect that people have problems, aren't all that interested in discussing them. They spend as little time as possible exploring problems directly; they just don't pay them much attention.

Asking questions to get more details

Quiet Leaders stay out of the details.

Another common approach to questioning is asking questions to get more details. "Tell me what's happening at work lately," we ask Yvonne. While this might be less negative than asking about problems, one of two things will happen here. First, we can find ourselves lost in all the details of Yvonne's projects, deadlines, and day-to-day life. Overloaded with information, we're now lost in the problem alongside Yvonne. Or second, through asking questions, we start to make connections ourselves about what Yvonne should do. And so we're back to giving advice. While this approach may be faster than straight-out advice (by asking questions your advice will be better targeted), you will still have to contend with the fact that the other person hasn't come up with the idea: they will now be arguing with you instead of energized by their own aha.

Quiet Leaders stay out of the details. They let the other person do all the thinking about their dilemma, while they think about something else entirely.

So if Quiet Leaders don't give advice, they don't focus on problems, and they don't ask about the details, what do they do?

Forcing people into action

Quiet Leaders don't rush people into action.

Well, you say, why not just ask Yvonne what action she might take to solve the issue? What about a question like "What are you going to do about this?" While this approach to questioning gets the other person doing the thinking, and it's certainly solutions-focused, this sort of question would basically annoy most people. It's a bit like a "Get out of jail" card in Monopoly—it's something you can only use in emergencies. Yvonne has come to you wanting your help, and you're replying by saying "What are you going to do about this?"

Quiet Leaders don't rush people into action. They focus on allowing people's thinking to take its natural course.

Telling people how to think

Quiet Leaders don't tell people how to think differently.

"Aha!" you say. "I have to ask Yvonne what her goals are, or what her vision of a perfect day at work is. Or maybe she has a confidence problem and should just believe in herself more . . ."

I have some bad news for you. The moment you come up with these ideas, your brain is making an incorrect assumption: that it's able to accurately calculate what Yvonne's brain needs to do to solve this problem. You are guessing the mental frame she should take on to process the situation more effectively. It's like when we say "Why don't you think about the big picture?" or "Why don't you be more positive about what you do have, rather than what you don't?" I personally find this approach mildly insulting.

Predicting the mental frame that will help Yvonne work through her challenge is about as easy as predicting the exact weather in a year. Even with all of Yvonne's life history, numerous psychological assessments, and supercomputers processing data about every neuron in her brain (if that were possible), you still would not be able to predict how Yvonne needed to think to solve her dilemma. Our brains are too complex. All you can do is tell Yvonne what *you* might do in a similar situation, which is exactly what we do without realizing it.

Quiet Leaders don't tell people how to think differently—not even if it's a great idea, such as focusing on their goals, becoming more relaxed, or being more positive. They know there is an easier way.

What Quiet Leaders do

We now know we're not going to give Yvonne advice, and we're not focused on her problems. We're not going to ask for details about her situation at work, and we're not suggesting other ways she could approach her dilemma.

Take a look at the diagram of Yvonne's dilemma below. If you take away the details and the problem, if you literally don't focus on those parts of the sentence (try covering these with two fingers right now), what's left to ask about?

"I'd really like to be **less stressed at work,** but it **just seems to get busier every week.**"

Have another look at the statement below now. If you don't ask about the detail or problem, the only thing left is the statement *"I'd really like to be . . ."*

"I'd really like to be **less stressed at work,** but it **just seems to get busier** every week."

In other words, the only other option is to help Yvonne recognize the qualities of her thinking itself. How better to help people make new connections, than to identify the patterns in their minds? In doing this we are helping Yvonne stand outside her own mental forest.

To put this simply, it means asking questions with the word

"thinking" in it. A great question to start might be "How long have you been thinking about this?" Then you might ask something like "How often do you think this each day?" Followed by "How important do you think this thought is?" then "How satisfied are you with the amount of thinking you have given this issue so far?"

I call these types of questions "thinking questions." These are one of the most useful tools I have ever found for improving performance.

Asking thinking questions means you are now focused on one thing: people's thinking. If people are being paid to think, isn't it about time we helped them improve their thinking?

Thinking questions ask about the nature of people's thinking, in ways that have them become more self-aware and take more responsibility.

More examples of thinking questions

"How long have you been thinking about this?"

"How often do you think about this?"

"How important is this issue to you, on a scale of one to ten?"

"How clear are you about this issue?"

"What priority is this issue for you in your work or life right now, top five, three, or top one?"

"What priority do you think it should be?"

"How committed to resolving this are you?"

"How motivated are you to resolving this?"

"Can you see any gaps in your thinking?"

"What impact is thinking about this issue having on you?"

"How do you react when you think that thought?"

"How do you feel about the resources you have put into this so far?"

"Do you have a plan for shifting this issue?"

"How clear is your thinking about the plan?"

"What are you noticing about your thinking?"

"What insights are you having?"

"How could you deepen this insight?"

"Would it be worth turning this insight into a habit?"

"Do you know what to do to turn this into a habit?"

"Are you clear about what to do next?"

"How can I best help you further?"

None of these questions focus on details or problems, nor do they tell people how to think. They get people to notice their own thinking. Something exciting happens when we ask these types of questions: People start to really think—in different ways, more clearly, and at a higher level. They become aware of the background of their thinking, and start to make new connections. Their eyes glaze over as they focus internally. Often they look up. In other words, they move to the reflection stage of the Four Faces of Insight. As a result, they can quickly move into the illumination phase, after just a few questions.

Let's go back to the story about standing at a corner with two sets of directions to get to the restaurant. Quiet Leaders don't say "The restaurant is that way." Nor do they take the map and work out the answer for you. They don't ask why you're having trouble working out the answer, nor do they get mad at you for being stuck. And, surprisingly, they don't ask leading questions like "Have you thought about checking the directions on the maps?"

Instead, Quiet Leaders ask questions that help you think more clearly. Questions like "What's your gut instinct here?" to which you answer, "I wonder if the restaurant might have moved—someone said it's been around a long time . . ." In a flash you think of checking the map dates. You now feel smarter, energized by your insights, and clear about what to do. Next time you get stuck anywhere you'll know to check the dates on any map you have, including your own mental ones.

Once you get used to this concept, asking thinking questions is significantly easier than trying to work out the answers for people. This approach is not just easier, it's more fun, inspires people into action, generates commitment, and transforms performance.

Other types of questions

Sometimes asking thinking questions may not bring about insights. People may not be willing to look deeply into their thinking. Or perhaps they can't get enough distance from their issue: they might be lost in the details, in an agenda, or a hot spot. Going back to the Choose Your Focus model, if thinking questions are not working, the next best questions to ask are about vision or planning. The more you can stay above the detail, problem, and drama, the quicker people will find solutions.

Imagine a colleague you manage says to you, "I don't know how to hit my targets this month." Assuming you'd established permission to go into this conversation, and had placed the person well, here are various ways you could choose to focus on the issue:

FOCUS OF YOUR QUESTION	EXAMPLE
Thinking:	How long have you been thinking about this?
Vision:	What do you want to achieve here?
Planning:	What's your plan for achieving these targets?
Detail:	Tell me about what you've done so far.
Problem:	What's in the way of hitting your targets?
Drama:	Tell me what will go wrong if you don't hit your targets.

Vision and planning questions are useful in many conversations. However, detail questions often end up taking time without adding much to a dialogue. Problem and drama questions send people down that slippery emotional slope into the problem.

If you're excited right now about this idea of thinking questions, you're in a great place, as the rest of this book will make this idea even clearer. For now let's illustrate how step four, Dance Toward Insight, fits together.

PUTTING PERMISSION, PLACEMENT, AND QUESTIONING TOGETHER

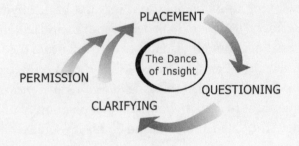

Figure 25, The Dance of Insight

Let's go back to the bank, where Sally went to have a difficult conversation with Paul.

> Sally: *Paul, I'd like to have a conversation about something that's a bit delicate to talk about. It might take us fifteen minutes or so—is this a good place and time? It's about that project that's been on both our minds a lot.*
>
> Paul: *Ahhh . . . I was focusing on something else, but okay, let's chat. Do you want to sit down?*
>
> Sally: *Thanks for making the time. I want to say up front that I know you're putting a lot of work into this project. I am not here to say you're doing anything wrong. But I'm keen to check in with how you are feeling about it all, and see if there is a way I could be of any help at all.*
>
> Paul: *Sure. Look, I want to make this project a success, but I have lots of other demands for my time this month. It's been pretty stressful.*
>
> Sally: *So could I help you think this through at all?*
>
> Paul: *Okay . . . Look, I know I need to get it done, I just seem to have so many different priorities. My time is spent jumping between my team, my emails, and this big project, but I'm not clear what to focus my time on.* [Paul has just expressed the

presenting dilemma, the challenge that's going on in his mind. And now Sally has a dilemma to interact with.]

Sally: *Sounds like you're not sure how to prioritize your attention.* [You've just seen the first example of "clarifying," which we cover next.]

Paul: *Yes, it definitely feels like that.*

Sally: *So what you're saying is you'd like to get this project done, but you don't seem to have the time, and you're not sure how to prioritize where you put your attention.* [She's just done some good ongoing placement, to describe where the conversation is up to. And as a result we've just completed one cycle of the Dance of Insight by going through permission, placement, questioning, and clarifying.]

Sally: *Can I ask a couple of more personal questions?* [Asking permission again, just to be safe, as she's going to get more personal by asking about his thinking now.]

Paul: *Sure.*

Sally: *How long has this been going on?* [She's asking about his thinking, to help Paul come up with his own insights, instead of asking about his problem or his schedule, or making a suggestion.]

Paul: *It's been, hmm . . . about a month or so.*

Sally: *And how do you feel about how much thought you've given to resolving this so far?*

Paul: *Well, let's see . . . it's like every day there in the background . . . look, I can see now.* [He's just had an aha: his brain has made a new set of connections.] *You know, that's what it is, I think I need to sit down and list all my projects, and put them in a clear order, and then block some time for them based on the priorities . . . thanks. That's been helpful.*

Sally: *Glad I could help. How do you feel about the project now?*

Paul: *Much better . . . I know this project is the number one priority, what I hadn't realized was I needed to look at the whole list of other projects and order everything properly so I know what to focus on second. Without this I think I've been floun-*

> *dering about somewhat, worried about what else I should be
> thinking about.*

Sally: *Is there anything else I could do to help you with this?*

Paul: *Could I talk over my priority list with you when it's done?
Might be useful to have someone to talk it over with.*

Sally: *Sure, do you want to book a time for that?*

In the conversation above, Sally wanted to know the project was going to go smoothly, and she sensed Paul needed to have a mental shift. Sally let Paul do all the thinking, while keeping him focused on solutions and stretching his thinking. She knew it would be better to help him think better, rather than tell him what to do.

Compare the conversation that happened to other ways this interaction could have gone. Sally could have:

- Avoided the issue all together. In this case Paul would struggle through and not perform as well. Perhaps Sally might feel guilty about avoiding the issue, and eventually blame Paul for low performance.
- Started a conversation about the problems with the project, resulting in their putting attention on the problems.
- Asked questions about the details of the project, and then told Paul what to do. Paul would then begrudgingly put this on his to-do list.

Using the Quiet Leadership approach, Sally handled the issue in minutes. Paul was energized by the conversation: the chemicals rushing through his brain and body from solving a dilemma that had chewed up energy for a month now spurred him into taking immediate action. Sally was also energized by the interaction, partly because some of Paul's newfound energy rubbed off on her, and partly as a result of knowing she'd made a difference.

Types of ahas that occur when we Dance Toward Insight

Sally couldn't have guessed Paul needed to create a priority list: the ahas people have are broad and unexpected. Using this model I have heard ahas like all of these: I should call that client; I need to apply the same plan from the launch to our new team meeting; I'm going to be nicer to myself; It's time I stopped putting that off; I must put a weekly meeting with everyone in my calendar; I am going to look after my top salesperson more; I need to get that health check up, it's affecting my confidence; I don't need to think about that for a month now.

There's one thing that's common to these ahas: the other person has improved their thinking. They've done this through one or more of the following mental processes:

- Noticing patterns in their thinking
- Lifting their thinking to a higher perspective
- Noticing qualities of their thinking itself, such as its poor quality, or a need for more focus on an issue
- Clarifying the importance of issues
- Reordering priorities
- Scheduling time more intelligently
- Paying more attention to certain thoughts
- Making firmer commitments
- Opening up their thinking

The ripple effects of helping someone resolve one dilemma, such as Paul seeing he needed to prioritize more thoroughly, can be substantial. Given the interlinked, complex nature of the brain, the new map Paul has created has a chance of being a long-term resource that can be applied to thousands of other situations.

Learning to ask thinking questions is a powerful resource for transforming performance. If your measurement is whether people take action, compared to telling people what to do, this approach saves a lot of time. And it doesn't just save energy, it creates energy.

■ ■ ■ ■ ■ ■ ■ EXERCISE STATION FOR ■ ■ ■ ■ ■ ■ ■ ■

Questioning

If you've had some insights about asking questions, this is an opportunity to deepen your thoughts by dwelling on them. Try writing down your insights, or talking to a friend about your thoughts, making a mind map, creating a collage, or anything that has you spend time deeply focused on your own insights about questioning.

Given this is such a central skill in this book, I recommend spending a whole week focused on the idea of thinking questions. You might like to read this chapter several times, to help you digest the ideas slowly. Try a few of the ideas, give this approach a go anywhere you can, talk to people about what you are doing. Anything you can do to create more connections to the concept of thinking questions is going to help this idea become a part of who you are.

_____

_____

_____

_____

_____

_____

CLARIFYING

*On the clarity of your ideas depends the scope
of your success in any endeavour.*

JAMES ROBERTSONS (1742–1814)

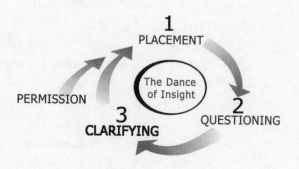

Figure 26, The Dance of Insight

Clarifying is the final element in the Dance of Insight. Once we have permission for a conversation, and place the other person, and ask a thinking question, we then clarify the answer to our question. When we clarify, we get to the bottom line in a conversation. We voice the essence of what's being said.

Something happened during a training I ran at IBM that illustrates the power of clarifying. I'd spent the first of two days teaching a group of facilitators the idea of dancing toward insights, using placement, thinking questions, and clarifying. The day had gone well but I felt I could have done better. I was wandering the halls afterward thinking about how I might run the next day differently, when I ran into one of the senior executives. He asked me how I thought my earlier session had gone, and I gave him my still-cloudy thoughts. I truly expected to get lots of feedback from him about the event, as well as suggestions about the event coming up. Instead he said just two words to me, which to this day stand as the most powerful piece of clarifying I've experienced. He said, "Change us." Then he smiled and walked away.

This executive, with the clarity of distance, had heard me say I was holding back on day one, something I wasn't conscious of. Through his clarifying, I saw what was going on at a deeper level. I raced back to my room with a million ideas on how to rework the next day, which went much better than the first.

Clarifying provides a missing link, an idea that completes a set of connections, so that the brain is ready for the next idea. The experience is like struggling to remember the title of a book: when suddenly the title comes barrelling in, you feel so much better.

When Sally said to Paul, "Sounds like you're not sure how to prioritize your attention," she was clarifying a long, complicated statement into a much clearer one. As a result, Paul saw his own thinking more clearly, and was thus able to see the gaps in his thinking for himself. Given that our working memory is small, simplifying complex ideas allows us to make connections to other ideas more easily. So the best clarifying involves a short, clear sentence of fewer than ten words.

Clarifying requires listening to people intently—though at a high level—listening for patterns rather than to every detail. You're well above the forest, trying to see which country the forest is in, or even which season. When you clarify, listen for:

- What is the person trying to say?
- What are they not saying?
- What is the emotional context inside what they are saying?
- What's "behind" their words—what do they really feel?
- What's the essence of what they're saying?
- What are they saying that they can't hear for themselves?

Here's a quick example:

Employee: *I spoke to each of the department heads and had a clear discussion about what I expected from them, including outlining what the specific objectives of this project are.*
Leader: *Sounds like you've been incredibly thorough.*

Clarifying isn't just repeating back what was said, in fewer words; that is known as "paraphrasing." Paraphrasing would be saying "So you spoke to everyone and made sure they all knew what to expect here." Clarifying adds something, it takes the conversation to a higher level. Clarifying is like sifting for gold in what someone says, which in this case was that the employee had been so thorough.

Imagine a peer at the start of a meeting says: "My day's been exhausting, I'm not sure I'll be able to focus here, my best friend's been crying on my shoulder all day, my partner yelled at me and I was late for three appointments." To clarify here you'd say "Sounds like today's been a real stretch for you." By offering a short response you let the other person know that you have listened, but you also add value by taking the drama out of the situation.

> Great clarifying is more like poetry than PowerPoint. You're capturing the essence of an idea and feeding it back in a way that makes people nod in agreement.

To clarify effectively, focus on the other person and what they might be learning. Thinking too much about what they're saying gets in the way, as does worrying about getting it perfect. Take time to fully consider their words, let them sink in, then trust your gut. If this sounds a lot like listening for potential, you're right: that's exactly what's needed to clarify well.

Some approaches to clarifying have more impact than others. Take a look at these two examples.

Employee: *I just got back from a meeting and heard that the board had noticed how well I was doing in my first quarter here.*

One leader's attempt at clarifying: "So you're pleased that the board has noticed your efforts." Will this have much of an impact on the employee? It's more like paraphrasing; the leader has not added much value here.

Another leader's attempt at clarifying: "Looks like you're having an impact around here." This would have a more positive impact—it's focused on the implications of what was said, and the leader is remembering to accentuate the positive.

If you want to know when you've clarified well, just look at people's heads. They will nod when you get it right! Even if what you say is not totally accurate, people will then clarify what you say. Either way, the conversation can then move forward.

Clarifying requires being prepared to take a risk and trusting your intuition. It's a high-level skill that requires some practice. Which, of course, brings us to an exercise station.

■ ■ ■ ■ ■ ■ ■ EXERCISE STATION FOR ■ ■ ■ ■ ■ ■ ■ ■

Clarifying

Imagine that you could capture the essence of conversations in just a few words, in a way that had people immediately feel better. That's the essence of good clarifying. To build this muscle takes stepping back from the details, listening to people as their potential, and focusing on emotions and learning. And, of course, being succinct, specific, and generous. Build your clarifying muscles by clarifying what people say to you for a few days. At the end of each day do some writing about what you notice. Clarify what you are noticing in your writing as well.

_____

_____

_____

_____

_____

_____

_____

PUTTING THE DANCE TOGETHER

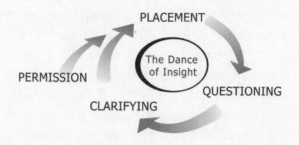

Figure 27, The Dance of Insight

Step four, Dance Toward Insight, is the central step in this book, with lots of different elements to it. I mentioned at the start of step four that I would help you understand each model on its own. Now that we've done that, let's see how it all fits together, with two different examples of conversations between Quiet Leaders and their employees.

Michelle and Peter

The first example is with Michelle and Peter from earlier on. Michelle, as the head of learning at a large consulting company, has just participated in a self-management workshop. Her boss, Peter, wants to see what impact the course has had, and to see if he can help her integrate what she learned.

Peter: *Can you chat for a few minutes now?*
Michelle: *Sure.*
Peter: *I'd like to get a handle on what you got out of that work-shop, to help you integrate your insights. I'd like to get a bit detailed—would now be a good time for you?* [Permission and placement together.]
Michelle: *Okay. Let me just send off this email so I can focus a bit . . . one sec . . . there, done. Let's talk.*

Peter: *Thanks. I am interested specifically in what you learned and how you think you might apply any insights you had, moving forward.* [More placement, being succinct and specific.] *I know some of the issues in the course could have been personal so I want you to know you don't have to tell me everything. Maybe we should just focus on the high points, are you okay with that?*

Michelle: *Sure.*

Peter: *So what was your biggest insight out of the workshop?* [Asking a high-level thinking question, rather than about all the details.]

Michelle: *There were lots . . . I found overall it was more involved than I'd expected. I guess I'd thought it would involve planning tools and techniques but instead we went into detail about how we manage each day. I did notice how useful it could be to actively plan my objectives for the day and the week . . . I haven't really been doing that . . .*

Peter: *So you're interested in developing a habit of setting daily and weekly goals?* [Clarifying.]

Michelle: *Yeah, I guess I am.*

Peter: *So as I said, I want to see how I can best help you build on this workshop, and you're saying the biggest insight was around setting daily and weekly goals.* [Ongoing placement summarizes where the dialogue is up to, which focuses both people on the intent of the conversation.] *So how could I best help you turn this insight into a habit?'* [Thinking question.]

Michelle: *I don't know . . . I guess if I could decide on three major goals to achieve each day, and then did these first . . . if I could make that a habit somehow . . . I think if I . . .* [She's just making some new connections.] *if I just put this into my calendar and focused on it for, say, a week, it would probably work. Could I use you as a sounding board and send you my list each day?*

Peter: *Sure, I'd be happy to help. Anything else you think I could do to help you here?*

Notice how little Peter had to do in the conversation. He just kept the conversation on target by getting permission for a deeper conversation first, then using placement, thinking questions, and clarifying, then back to placement. I'll put the next statement in bold because it's such a central point in this whole book:

Peter's whole focus here was helping his staff member think more clearly, more deeply, more effectively, while simply staying out of the way.

Peter achieved a big objective in just a few minutes: He wanted to make sure Michelle had the best chance of developing new habits out of the workshop. After a few days of seeing how she was going with this new idea, by following up with her (which we'll read about in the next step), he might see she's now taken on this habit, and is ready to stretch further. In conversations that take hardly any time, he's improving her thinking, and no doubt her performance will be impacted as a result.

Mike and Sam

If you read my first book, *Personal Best*, you might remember Mike. He learned a lot about himself through being coached, and at the end of a few months of coaching he'd become more self-aware and was taking more responsibility for his impact on others.

Mike is now the CEO of his firm, and Sam is the CFO reporting to him. Sam has come to Mike to ask for help with a business unit. Here's how the conversation might go if Mike used the models in this book.

Sam: *We need to get this new division going but I just don't think we have the right people.*

Mike: *Do you want to talk about this in a bit of detail right now?* [Getting permission.]

Sam: *Sure.*

Around this point in a conversation most leaders make suggestions, ask questions so they can then make suggestions, or try and drill down into the problem. Look what Mike does instead.

Mike: *I don't want to tell you what to do with this division; it's one of your teams and it's up to you to make the decisions, but I'd be happy to see if I can help you develop your thoughts further and see if any new ideas come up. Is that good with you?* [Placement.]

Sam: *Sounds good. Let me tell you what's been happening . . .* [Notice that people usually want to go into the detail, and the role of the leader is often to lift the conversation to a higher level.]

Mike: *Before we go there, can I take us in a slightly different direction here? I don't think first off I need to know all the details, I'd rather start with understanding your thinking and see if I can work with that.*

Sam: *Okay . . . I guess. Let's give it a go.*

Mike: *So you said "We need to get this new division going"—how long have you been thinking about this?* [Thinking question.]

Sam: *I don't know, maybe . . . hmm . . . must be since we bought in that new unit and took over the finances from the other team, maybe a couple of years now.*

Mike: *Quite a while then.* [Mike has just clarified, which completes one cycle of the Dance of Insight.]

Sam: *Yeah, I guess so . . . I hadn't noticed it had been there so long until now.* [Sam's already making connections that this has been going on a long time; in his mind he's building commitment to action.]

Mike: *So what you're saying is, we need to get this new division going, you're not sure you have the right people, and you've been thinking about it for quite a while now.* [Placement.] *And how often are you thinking about it, how many times a day or week?* [Another thinking question, deepening awareness.]

Sam: *Don't know . . . maybe it's there every day, yeah, I'd say it's there four or five times a day, in the back of my mind.* [Sam's just had another pretty important crystalization of his thoughts, that this issue is taking up a lot of his mental space.]

Mike: *So it's taking up lots of focus then.* [Clarifying.]

Sam: *I'm just not sure what to do, though, whether to just hire more people or do another audit, or what. What are your thoughts?* [People often try to pass the buck back to the leader when they find they have to really think.]

Mike: *Can we keep going and see what ideas you can come up with first? If there's anything I want to add I might do that afterward.* [The buck is firmly passed back to Sam.]

Sam: *Yeah, okay.*

Mike: *Let's see where we are. You really want to get this new division going, but are not sure if you have the right people, you've been thinking about it for a while, and it's taking up a lot of your mental energy every day.* [Placement is important here. The conversation could go so many ways right now, on tangents, sideways, backward, or even stop because it feels too hard. In this case the placement is going to help Mike himself make sure he asks the best possible questions.]

Mike: *So how do you feel about what you've done to shift this so far?* [Notice how it's possible to ask about someone's thinking about the details, without getting into the details themselves—quite a useful mini skill.]

Sam: *Now that I can see how much mental energy it's taking up, I feel like I should tackle this head-on a lot more.* [Sam's made some deeper connections now.]

Mike: *So you want to make this a priority now?* [Clarifying.]

Sam: *Definitely.*

Mike: *How could I best help you think this through? Do you know what you need to do and want to make some deadlines with me, or are you still in brainstorming phase? How could I best help you think from here?*

Around the end of this dialogue there was noticeable phase change. Sam's had an aha, which was "It's time I made this a priority." Immediately after this insight the conversation goes in a new direction. You could say it's gone to a new level. The current reality of Sam's thinking has been explored, and now they are going to explore alternatives for how to move this issue forward.

Let's take a moment to recap on the Dance of Insight, to help crystalize what we've covered so far. The Dance of Insight is a framework for having conversations that help people think better, without telling them what to do. The elements within this model can improve the effectiveness of many types of conversations. We've seen that the Dance of Insight is cyclical in nature. A dilemma comes up. You get permission for a new conversation. You place the person so you're both thinking from the same perspective, then you ask a thinking question to get their mind noticing their own thinking patterns. Then you clarify their answers, and you're back to placement again (or permission if you're getting more personal). Then you're back to a thinking question, then clarifying, etc.

While in real conversation it's not quite as step-by-step as this, there is definitely a pattern that, if followed, helps conversations go deeper. Even roughly following these steps can make a dramatic difference to the quality of dialogues.

Here are a couple of high-level insights that came to me through watching people learn these skills.

1. When people feel lost in a conversation, it's usually a result of a lack of placement. If placement feels annoying somehow, remember you're telling people about themselves, something which is rarely boring.
2. When people are lost in the details or problems, I can pinpoint the exact question the leader asked that sent the conversation off the rails. People answer the question we ask.
3. When people are not clear what the central issue is, the leader has almost always failed to do enough clarifying.

In summary, the Dance of Insight is central to being a Quiet Leader. It's about getting permission before getting personal, then making sure you're both on the same page before asking a question, then asking questions that create new maps in people's minds. As you quietly facilitate this dance, you'll see people's faces changing as they move from the awareness of a dilemma, to reflecting, to having an illumination, and then being ready to take action. Having these dance steps in your repertoire as a leader will make a tremendous difference to the quality of your people's thinking, and therefore their performance.

■ ■ ■ ■ ■ ■ ■ EXERCISE STATION FOR ■ ■ ■ ■ ■ ■ ■

Dance of Insight

Take a week to keep working through the steps in the Dance of Insight. Practice getting permission every time you feel slightly uncomfortable about any topic. Use placement in every conversation that's slightly complex or challenging. Use thinking questions every opportunity you can. Try clarifying complex sentences and ideas into just a few words that contain the essence of what people are trying to communicate. You may start to find yourself naturally putting the steps together and going back to placement every time you get a bit lost. Hardwiring the ideas in step four is going to be useful before we move on to step five.

If you have someone to work with, try practicing on each other. You could describe a dilemma you are having and let the other person use the four steps to help you think it through, then swap roles. You could do this in small groups to learn from each other. Trying these models live, even as a practice exercise with a friend, is going to make a big difference compared to just reading the book and thinking it through.

_____

_____

_____

_____

_____

CREATE NEW THINKING

What we think, we become.

GAUTAMA BUDDHA (563 BC TO 483 BC)

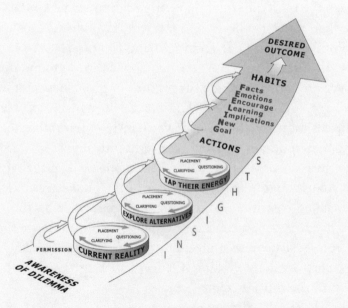

Figure 28, The CREATE Model

Dance Toward Insight is the biggest step in this book. It illustrates how to have conversations so that other people have insights. While the Dance of Insight is a circular model, you don't just keep spinning in the same circles. Like an electron that jumps to a higher orbit around the nucleus of an atom as it gets more energized, as people have insights, new types of conversations naturally emerge. For example, once someone has the "aha" that they need to make a project a priority, the next conversation will be about how to achieve that, followed by how to make sure it definitely happens. If you didn't have the CREATE model, you might help people have lots of good ideas, but not necessarily do anything with them.

The picture above gives you a sense of how steps four and five fit together. As you can see, each of the three parts of the CREATE model has the Dance of Insight at its core.

The first element of the CREATE model is to explore the Current Reality for someone, the reality of their thinking itself. At this point, people become aware of their dilemma, they reflect, and then, if you ask the right questions, have an insight of some kind.

We then move to the second element, Explore Alternatives. By this point people have had an insight and want to *do something* with the insight, but are not yet sure what. So we throw around different ideas. We might make gentle suggestions or give clues to other perspectives or approaches here. This stage helps ensure people don't take the easiest path when they have an insight, but rather that they find the best option for moving an insight into action.

The third element of the CREATE model is Tap their Energy. People are now in the motivation state of the Four Faces of Insight: They are energized about doing something, but we know this energy won't last. So we help people take tangible actions to move their insights from delicate new connections to something more likely to become a part of their thinking. Or in plain English, we're helping people turn their insights into habits.

Let's look at each of these elements and explore some examples of dialogues. I won't give you exercise stations for each element, just one to tie it all together at the end.

CURRENT REALITY

The beginning is the most important part of the work.

PLATO (CIRCA 400 BC)

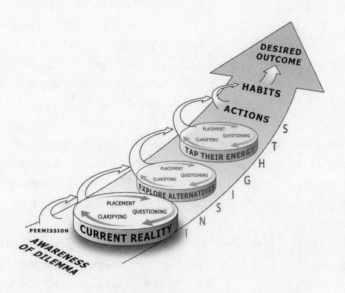

Figure 29, Current Reality

When you want to improve someone's thinking, the best place to start is at the current reality. Starting at this point enables people to reflect on their own thinking, which as we've seen is a fast way to generate insights.

When we ask about the current reality we ask people to step back from their own thinking and notice its nature: to become scientists of their own thinking. This is also similar to the Buddhist notion of mindfulness,[42] the concept of the observer noticing what's going on without being attached to any of it.

Helping someone identify the current reality of their thinking, without any value judgments, allows them to make new maps to self-correct this thinking. As a result, people make their own decisions about what to do next. Their thinking has literally been improved, and they've quite possibly developed useful new wiring to call on again.

Let's explore this from a scientific perspective. Our thoughts are a form of energy, just like light and sound. If we want to understand the nature of any type of energy there are standard scientific questions to ask. It's helpful to know the energy's frequency, which is how often it cycles during a specific time interval. Also its duration, which is the length of each cycle, and its intensity, which is the amount of energy within each cycle. It will be helpful to understand the impact the energy has on us, such as sound waves versus gamma waves. Then there are issues like longevity, quality, and comparative strengths to other energies.

The more we understand an energy source, the more we can see its relevance to us and therefore know what to do with it. This is true whether we're talking about the discovery of a new elementary particle, or a pattern in our thinking we had not yet noticed consciously.

Joe is a thirty-five-year-old financial controller in a government welfare office. Joe's been with the organization for eight years, and is one of the youngest senior managers in the department. He's in charge of a team of twenty people, who between them manage the finances of the whole state agency.

Imagine that Joe reports to you, and during a weekly one-on-one meeting he says, "I don't know how I'm going to get all my reports done this month." Before reading this book, your normal tendency might have been to throw out ideas like *"Why don't you use your planner and schedule your time more carefully?"* or *"Have you looked closely at your priorities?"* or *"Have you thought about . . ."* These questions are guesses about how to help Joe.

There are plenty of opportunities to make suggestions and share your ideas as a leader within the CREATE model. However, the best place to make suggestions is during the Explore Alternatives phase.

Now that you've read this book, instead of telling Joe what you think he should do, now you might say, *"Do you want to talk about that a bit more?"* [Permission.]; then: *"Let's see if I can help you think this through a bit."* [Placement.]; then: *"How long have you been thinking about this"* (A thinking question about the current reality). Then you can ask more questions about his thinking itself.

You might prefer to call the first element of step five "cognitive reality," because we are specifically identifying the landscape of a person's thinking rather than the landscape of their issue. These two questions should make this idea clearer:

- A question about the current reality of Joe's thinking: *"How important to you is getting all these reports in on time, on a scale of one to ten?"*
- A question about the current reality of Joe's issue: *"What are the reports you need to get done and by when?"*

People also find the CREATE model very helpful in situations where you do need to get detailed. Working at a detail level, it's useful to start with the current reality of a situation so you can see the landscape clearly; it's helpful to then explore alternatives for action rather than launching too quickly in the most obvious direction; and once you've set a course it's a good idea to tap all the energy available. I'm going to focus on how to use the CREATE model to improve thinking, rather than how you might use it to improve, say, project management. You may find many other ways you can use this model, it's just where I am choosing to focus. I'll explore other ways the model can be used in the last section of the book, for example, when working with teams.

Example questions for exploring the Current Reality

I find we need to ask at least five questions in this phase before people have any insights, though the range is usually six to ten. I have created a list of the common questions to ask. It's not a complete list, there are many variations on these themes, and I still come across great new questions even now.

"How long have you been thinking about this, in days, weeks, months, or years?"

"How often do you think about this, how many times each hour, day, or week?"

"How long do you think about it, when you do think about it, in minutes or hours?"

"How important is this issue to you, on a scale of one to ten?

"Is this in your top three, five, or ten priorities right now?"

"How committed to changing this issue are you, on a scale of one to ten?"

"How do you feel about the thinking time you have given this so far?"

"What are your main insights about this issue up to now?"

"On a scale of one to ten, how confident are you that you have all the information you need to act?"

"What's the insight brewing at the back of your mind?"

If you can recall these types of questions, you might find it easier to focus on the person you're speaking to, so some people like to cut out or copy this list and put it on the wall or memorize it. With these questions in mind, here are a few nuances to be aware of around this process: the importance of metrics; not to give up too quickly; to watch people's faces; and above all, to trust your gut.

Numbers count

When we want people to have an aha, simplifying their ideas is a big help. A great way to do this is by defining the strength of any concept in number form. There are two main reasons for this.

First, defining our thoughts and feelings in numbers makes us think more deeply. Ask someone "What priority is your health, as a number, compared to everything else in your life?" and they have to stop, reflect, be really honest with themselves, and then give you a precise answer. This gives the specific mental circuits involved much more attention than if you asked "How do you feel about your health?"

Second, because numbers are simple, our working memory can hold them more easily in our conscious mind, and therefore more easily see connections to other concepts. For example, you might sense that you're not focused enough on a specific project. If you had to define the importance of that project, you might see it was number one. If you then had to define what number priority it was in your schedule, which might be fifth, the disconnect would clearly stand out.

There are many ways you can bring numbers into a conversation. Let's say someone's central issue is balsamic vinegar. (I'm not crazy—someone, somewhere, manages people who make the stuff.) To help a manager identify the importance of balsamic vinegar, you could ask:

> "How important is balsamic vinegar here on a **scale of one to ten**?"
> "Where is balsamic vinegar in a list of importance, **number one, top three, top five, bottom five**?"
> "What **percent of the time** do you use balsamic vinegar?"
> "How much of a disaster would it be if you had no balsamic vinegar, on the **Richter scale**?" [You can get creative and have fun with metrics too.]

Numbers count (sorry). Use them whenever you can, to help people gain more clarity.

Don't be afraid to dig around a bit—ask at least five questions

While training others in this model, I've noticed that people are inclined to be lazy: they stop after just two or three current reality questions. Maybe they didn't want to stretch people too much. It's rare that people have an insight just by being asked how often they think about something and for how long. Remember from the start of the book the importance of being comfortable making people feel uncomfortable. Ask permission a lot, but get in and ask a lot of questions.

Watch their face or listen to their tone

The Four Faces of Insight model is useful here. People's inner processing shows up on their faces, or if you're on the phone, in their tone of voice. You can watch and listen for clues as to whether you're getting warmer or colder with your questions. When people get close to an insight they go quiet, which they need to do to come up with new connections. Give them space to do this. When they have an aha you can see it written all over their face, or you'll hear their voice shift to a higher pitch.

Trust your gut

I've left the most important message about the current reality phase until last. Start the conversation with several easy questions to help people reflect more. I have given you lots of examples of these already. After a few questions you'll hear where their energy is going, and if you listen carefully, you'll sense the next question to ask. Follow their words, their energy, and trust your instincts. If someone says "I feel like I've had *this* dilemma before," with emphasis on the word "this," you might say, "Sounds like it's not a new issue . . . how many times has this dilemma come up in your life?" That question wasn't on my list of great current reality questions, it was just my curiosity about the person's thinking based on what was said.

The CREATE model is a guide. It will only work if you listen to your natural curiosity and ask questions about where you sense the person's energy is going. If you trust your gut you might find yourself coming up with a great question such as "Do you have the answer already and just want to check it with me?" Sometimes this is exactly what's going on for people, and just by speaking an idea out loud they're able to move forward quickly.

Above all, trust your gut, and have fun with it.

EXPLORE ALTERNATIVES

*The test of a first-rate intelligence is the ability to hold two opposed
ideas in mind at the same time and still retain the ability to function.*

F. Scott Fitzgerald (1896–1940)

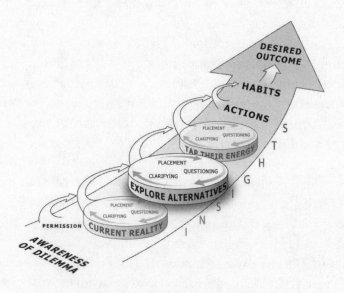

Figure 30, Explore Alternatives

It's clear when it's time to explore alternatives. It's when someone's
had an illumination and is full of energy—when Joe has seen that he
needs to put more time into planning, but hasn't yet worked out how.

When people have an aha they are energized, they feel inspired to
take action. However, the first actions that they come up with are
often what they are most comfortable with, not necessarily the best
ideas. When we explore alternatives we open people up to possibilities. We stretch them a little.

This part of the CREATE model usually requires less effort for
both people than the current reality part does, and it tends to be
faster. All we're doing is putting forward various possible ways to

move an insight forward. And, by now, people are energized by an insight.

Moving to the explore alternatives phase means asking people to think more deeply, so we need to make sure we establish permission to do this. We won't tend to ask permission as explicitly as we do when starting a dialogue; it's subtler here. It might be a simple question like "Are you okay to throw around some ideas about this with me now?"

Once we've got permission, again we use a bit of placement. We might just say "So let's explore lots of possible ideas here." We'll then ask a question to get them thinking, clarify their answer, and go back to placement. Overall the explore alternatives phase is less structured than the current reality phase; all the elements of the Dance of Insight are still there, just less explicitly.

Example questions for Exploring Alternatives

Questions to ask in this phase include:

"What are some possible paths we could take from here?"
"Do you want to explore a few different ideas for how to move this forward?"
"How could I best help you from here?"
"How do you think we might move this insight forward?"
"What are some different ways we could tackle this?"
"Can you see some different angles we could look at this from?"

When you are exploring alternatives, stay light and try out lots of ideas, without being attached to any. Be flexible and open-minded. Listen for people's energy, instead of worrying about what the right answer is.

Let's see how this looks in Joe's situation. Joe's had an insight about needing to redo his priorities. The explore alternatives phase could go like this:

Leader: *Are you open to exploring a few ideas about how to prioritize your work?* [Permission.]

Joe: *Sure, I'll take all the help I can get here.*

Leader: *So let's step back for a moment and look at a few different ideas.* [Placement.] *What would you normally do when you want to prioritize thoroughly?* [Asking him about his thinking—in this case, about the existing mental software he can apply to this challenge.]

Joe: *I don't know, maybe I just do a quick mental calculation, it happens fast.*

Leader: *So it's all in your head then.* [Clarifying.]

Joe: *Yep. I think this one needs some special attention. . . . I can't seem to work it out in my head.*

Leader: *Okay, so what are some other ideas that might work here, that might help you prioritize?*

Joe: *Hmm . . . maybe write a list and leave it for a day?*

Leader: *That could work, are you open to a few ideas I have as well?* [Asking permission to make suggestions.]

Joe: *Sure.*

Leader: *It might be worth talking to a few people to get other perspectives, or it might be worthwhile doing a spreadsheet and working this out logically, applying some numbers to your projects, you could look at things like . . .*

Joe: *You know what, I think I want to do that, I'm going to do a spreadsheet here. That's going to work for me. I just need a way of focusing in and spending ten minutes being logical about all my stuff—it's all a bit messy in my head right now.*

Leader: *Sounds like a plan.*

Next time Joe hits a similar roadblock, he'll probably sit down and think through a difficult issue by building a spreadsheet. Joe now has the possibility of a new habit, some wiring he can draw on to help him perform better in future decision making.

Filters and agendas

When we start to help people think through alternatives, we need to be aware of our own filters and agendas. If Joe wanted to throw away the idea of reports forever, your agenda might come up, that of wanting him to work within standard protocols. There's nothing wrong with this; our agendas at times are important. Just disclose them, and then discuss what's best.

Gently posing suggestions

During this phase, take advantage of opportunities to offer examples, alternatives, and suggestions. These can help people think in different ways. Joe's insight was that he needed to look at his priorities more closely. If, when you explored alternatives, all he came up with was "Think about my priorities," you could throw in suggestions like doing an "urgent versus important" analysis, or some kind of chart, or asking others on his team for help.

If you put ideas forward as possibilities and allow people to make the decision about what works for them, you can throw in lots of great tools, approaches, resources, and suggestions. Then you can help people decide which would be the most useful approach, not just the easiest. Exploring alternative ways to take action after having an insight, instead of just going with first ideas, can be a big help in transforming performance. Just remember not to be too attached to any ideas, as all our brains are different.

TAP THEIR ENERGY

It is the nature of thought to find its way into action.

CHRISTIAN NEVELL BOVEE (1820–1904)

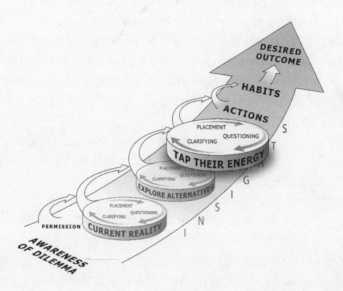

Figure 31, Tap Their Energy

Let's take a high-level view of the three elements of the CREATE model. The current reality phase usually takes the most time and focus. Exploring alternatives takes less time and effort. The "tap their energy" phase has a life of its own. The energy released by making big sets of new connections spurs people into action and all the leader has to do is gently nudge people to keep them on the right track.

Remember that the motivation people feel is driven by neurotransmitters that are released through the creation of new maps; however, the motivation lasts only a short time. With the number of ideas we process every day, if we don't anchor an insight in reality, our insights can easily get buried in our physical, mental, and digital inboxes. So the leader's role here is largely to make sure actions definitely happen, in several ways—including helping the other person be more specific about an action, and by putting some deadlines in place. As my friend and colleague from NYU Elizabeth Guilday says, "Specificity equals response-ability."

Let's go back to Joe. We moved to the tap their energy phase when Joe decided to create a spreadsheet. Here's how this might go. First, we'd subtly establish permission, with something like "Are you okay if I stretch you a little here?" If he was okay with this we might say "When will you do this by?" or "Do you need to put that in your calendar at all?" Or we might ask if he'd send the spreadsheet in to us. We're all busy; without a structure to ensure an action is done, our important but not-so-urgent insights may get parked behind other priorities.

There are four main issues to be aware of here: helping people be more specific; setting deadlines; reporting back; and doing something tangible.

Get specific while their energy is still flowing

I had an insight today about creating an online questionnaire for leaders in a new training program. While it was fresh in my thinking I wrote out a big list of questions. If I'd put the idea aside and tried to write it up tomorrow, it might take a few minutes to find my other notes, then a few minutes of going back over my thoughts, then more time to struggle through the exercise of writing up the questions. Given that I would need maybe thirty minutes to complete the exercise, there's a chance it might get bumped by more urgent projects. Yet writing up the questions took only three minutes doing it right away. I was energized by the insight, I had mental momentum around this issue, and the ideas were fresh and clear in my mind. My point is: Get people to flesh out their ideas while they are fresh. It will increase the chances of real change.

Create deadlines while people are more likely to commit

Once I had my list of questions in the example above, I knew I needed a specific deadline for this project, otherwise it might slip away. So I decided to have the questions up on a Web form within three days. As a result of a specific deadline, my insight was far more likely to become a reality. Asking people that "by when" question while they are still energized by their idea means you're more likely to get a firm commitment. And once people have made a promise to themselves or others, they're far more likely to carry out their action.

Reporting back raises the odds substantially

The act of having to report to someone increases the amount of energy we give an idea in our minds; it makes us take an idea more seriously. Other people's impressions of us are important—we don't like to disappoint. You can tap into this quirk just by asking Joe to email his spreadsheet to you. We'll explore this whole concept more in step six, Follow Up.

Doing any kind of tangible activity linked to the insight

Writing an action down—for example "Make my decision on a spreadsheet"—makes that action more likely to happen. And it's not just because the action is now in our calendar, though of course that helps too. Applying any kind of physical activity to an insight strengthens the circuits holding the insight in place. Physical activities include talking, writing, reading, drawing, and filing; anything that focuses our attention on an insight for an amount of time.

From a neuronal perspective, taking an action rather than just thinking about something creates a raft of other connections that deepens the weave of links holding the original insight in place. The act of paying attention to the thought "I will do a spreadsheet" for one minute while writing it down, as opposed to just thinking about doing that spreadsheet for six seconds, increases the connections involved in this circuit by a significant factor. Attention creates new circuits.[43] As Jeffrey Schwartz says, "The power of attention . . . allows us to change—in scientifically demonstrable ways—the systematic functioning of our own neural circuitry."

Writing down the action "do a spreadsheet" means we now have connections between the action and our motor centers, from the physical act of picking up a pen and writing. We also now have links to our memory centers: We can remember writing the action down, as well as where we left it, how we wrote it, even how we felt when we wrote it. All these parts of your brain now have links to your original insight. It's like a cotton sheet with five hundred threads per square inch versus one with two hundred—the weave is tighter as a result of all this activity linked to our insight.

Example questions for Tapping Their Energy

"Shall we focus on x and get more detailed on that?"

"How can I best help you think through how to make this work?"

"Do you want to think through how to make this happen?"

"What specifically would you do in this situation?"

"When do you think you might do this by?"

"How can I best support you to turn this insight into a habit?"

"Do you want to take some kind of specific action around this?"

Notice that the language in these questions is unobtrusive and gentle. We're not saying "What are you going to do about that?" We want to stretch people, but also be sensitive. A new habit is a delicate and fragile creation, and just like a young seedling, it needs a warm and nurturing environment in which to grow.

Let's move now to putting this whole model together with some example dialogues.

PUTTING THE CREATE MODEL TOGETHER

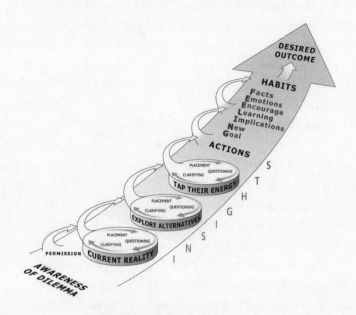

Figure 32, The CREATE Model

While the CREATE model describes three distinct phases in a dialogue, in real conversations it's not as linear as that. We usually start with the current reality, but may then move up and down between the other phases. Once we've tapped the energy for one insight, we might go back to the current reality on another aspect of an issue. Although it's not perfectly linear, my experience is that when people understand these three phases they can more easily sense which phase to move to next.

Let's put the current reality, explore alternatives, and tap their energy phases together with an example drawn from a sales performance issue. A common dilemma here is "I really want to improve my team's sales but I am just not sure what to do." Leaders often take this question as a signal to tell people what to do; the CREATE model describes a whole other approach.

As we get into the dialogue, don't be put off by the words the characters use. If the words don't feel like you, remember that everyone using the Six Steps will find different words they are comfortable with for the same concepts. So focus more on the process. Also some people have said that these conversations sound "unreal," that they're not the kind of discussion they ever hear at work. My response is that just because people don't communicate like this now doesn't mean they can't.

The dialogue below is between two senior leaders in a magazine publishing group. Ellen is the general manager in charge of performance across several high-profile magazines. She manages Sue, who looks after the advertising sales teams of several magazines. I have taken out any small talk that might happen prior to the dilemma being clarified, to shine attention on the central models here.

> Sue: *I really want to get our sales going but everyone's in a slump right now. I could do with your help on this.*
>
> Ellen: *No problem. Look, rather than me tell you what I think you should do, let me throw you a pile of questions and see what ideas come up. You say you really want to improve your team's sales but everyone's in a slump right now. So, when you say you "really" want to get their sales going, what do you mean by "really"? How important is this to you on a scale of one to ten?*
>
> Sue: *It's an eleven. No, really, it's ten out of ten, it's taking up my whole brain, I can't focus on much else. We've still got ten weeks left in this budget period but we need to make up a lot of ground to hit our targets.*
>
> Ellen: *So this is your number one priority then.*
>
> Sue: *Absolutely.*
>
> Ellen: *Let me see if I've got you . . . you really want to get your sales going, but everyone's in a slump, and it's now your number one priority. So how clear is your thinking here—are you totally lost, or do you know what you need to do but just need support? How clear are you about the next steps?*
>
> Sue: *I just have no idea at all now. I have tried incentives, I have tried more team meetings, I have tried subtle threats—nothing seems to work.*

Ellen: *Sounds like you're all out of ideas.*

Sue: *You got it.*

Ellen: *So you've got this project that's a number one priority but you're all out of ideas . . . How do you feel about the amount of thinking time you've given this issue so far, given it's your number one priority?*

Sue: *That's a good question . . . I guess I've been mulling over the same ideas for a while now . . .*

Ellen: *How long for exactly?*

Sue: *Hmm . . . maybe four or five months.*

Ellen: *And how often do you estimate you've been thinking about this issue, over that time?*

Sue: *I guess it's there every day, maybe a few dozen times a day. Wow, I've really been thinking about this a lot . . . I wonder . . .*

Sue goes quiet for a moment and reflects here, then bursts out with this.

Sue: *You know what, I just had an insight: I keep thinking about how I need to get the team going to hit these target, but I don't think the team buys into the targets themselves . . . I bet they don't even know what they are. I think I need to get everyone more on board. It feels like I'm the only one doing the thinking about this out of the whole team.*

Ellen: *Sounds like a useful insight!*

We've just got to the end of the current reality phase. There's a noticeable shift in the conversation now.

Ellen: *Do you want to explore this idea a bit further, see if I can help you clarify how to best approach the team here?* [Getting permission to move to the explore alternatives phase.]

Sue: *Sure, why not.*

Ellen: *So you want to get the team more on board with these targets.* [The placement this time takes off from the start of the explore alternatives phase.] *What are some different ways you might do this?*

Sue: *I don't know, maybe have a meeting but . . . during meetings no one seems to say much. Plus, I've tried that already.*

Ellen: *Let's explore a few ideas then. What else could you do?*

Sue: *I could maybe have some one-on-one time with a few of the key players and see what they think.*

Ellen: *Great, any other ideas?*

Sue: *I don't know, what do you think?*

Ellen: *Well, I don't want to tell you how to do your job, but a couple of possibilities that come to mind might be to let this come out at an informal event, or to have some smaller group gatherings where people might feel more free to talk. There's lots of different ways to do this.* [Remember that the explore alternatives phases is a great time to throw in good ideas as a manager. The key is to be unattached, so that people are more likely to feel an idea is their choice.]

Sue: *You know what, I've got it—it would be great to have a social event and broach this over a few drinks. I've wanted to have some time out with everyone for a while, so this could achieve a few things at once. Excellent idea, thanks.*

We've now completed the explore alternatives phase, as Sue has made a decision about what she wants to do. It's worth going a bit further though, to increase Sue's chances of success.

Ellen: *Sounds like you've got your answer. Can I ask a couple more questions to see if I can help any further?* [Permission to move to the tap their energy phase.]

Sue: *Sure.*

Ellen: *What do you need to do to make sure your event is a success?*

Sue: *Good question . . . I suppose I'm a bit worried about timing . . . and that people won't come.*

Ellen: *What do you need to do to make sure they do?*

Sue: *Well, I suppose the main things are to make sure it's an activity during work, to let people know it's required, but at the*

Ellen:
Sue:
    same time get the message out that it will be fun. I might ask some of my team for ideas, they're good with this.

Ellen: *Sounds great. What's your specific target then?*

Sue: *I do need a deadline . . . I'll commit to getting an email out to everyone within forty-eight hours and to have an event booked within the week. What do you think?*

Ellen: *Well, what do you think? Is your thinking really clear that this is all it will take to ensure the event is a success?*

Sue: *Now that I think about it, it might be useful to get some help calling everyone, not just emailing . . . I'll ask one of my people to do a phone around as well.*

Ellen: *Sounds like a great idea. How do you feel about this whole situation now?*

Sue: *Much better—thanks so much for your support.*

There are a few insights I'd like to point out here. First, the conversation gets slightly less structured as you move through the phases. While permission and placement are still being used, it's not quite as cyclical as we move up into the later parts of the dialogue. Second, we do get a bit detailed as we go on, but it's detailed about alternative solutions, about actions Sue's going to take. Third, consider the difference that the tap their energy questions made here: While Sue had a useful insight, if Ellen hadn't stretched her thinking, she may not have realized she needed a deadline, or had the insight to ask for help to phone around. There's a fair chance as a result that the meeting may not happen.

By using the CREATE model here, Ellen has improved Sue's thinking, without telling her what to do in any way. The impact on the organization of this one conversation could be substantial. In just a five-minute conversation, the possibility of a real transformation in performance has opened up.

Quiet Leaders create new thinking in the people they manage. They do this by following all the five steps we have covered so far: By thinking about thinking, by listening for potential, by speaking with intent, and by dancing toward insight. They do this by starting conversations with identifying the landscape of a person's thinking, widely exploring alternatives for action, and tapping into people's energy and motivations.

However, there's one last thing that Quiet Leaders do as well; they follow up.

■ ■ ■ ■ ■ ■ ■ **EXERCISE STATION FOR** ■ ■ ■ ■ ■ ■ ■

CREATE New Thinking

The CREATE model is the central model that ties together the first five of the Six Steps to Transforming Performance. The CREATE model describes the path of least resistance, the shortest and easiest way to get from wanting to help someone think better to having a real impact on their performance. It's also quite a conceptual, high-level idea. So a useful action here is to do something tangible yourself to anchor this model into your thinking. Some possible ways you could do this include explaining it to others, or creating your own diagram of the model, or doing some writing. Anything you can do to give the circuits holding this concept in your thinking some attention will make a difference.

_____

_____

_____

_____

_____

_____

_____

_____

_____

_____

FOLLOW UP

Cells that fire together, wire together.

CARLA SCHATZ (1992)

Facts

Emotions

Encourage

Learning

Implications

New

Goal

Figure 33, The FEELING Model

Using the CREATE model with someone whose thinking is unclear helps them have useful insights, and then commit to undertaking specific actions to bring these insights into reality. However, if we don't follow up, these actions may not have the long-term impact on performance that's possible.

Let's go back to Joe. He was initially worried about getting all his reports done this month. His leader used the CREATE model to generate new thinking. This new thinking was in the form of a new insight, "I'm going to build a spreadsheet for my various projects to analyze their importance." If you just left it at that, my guess is there would be only 50 percent as much chance[44] that Joe would do the spreadsheet, compared to if Joe knew you would be following up with him. So following up with Joe is obviously a way of ensuring he's acted on his good intentions. However, making sure an action is done is only a small part of the value of following up. The big reason to follow up after creating new thinking is to support the creation of new long-term habits that will improve people's performance.

We explored how we create new habits in the chapter It's Easy to Create New Wiring at the start of the book. We discovered that we create new connections all the time, and that it's not too hard to turn these connections into circuits that stay with us for some time. What's needed is attention, time, repetition and positive feedback.

Let's go back a couple of steps. The actions people set come out of insights they have. These insights are generated in a moment of illumination. At the moment of illumination a new set of connections between our neurons, a new map, comes into existence that was not there before, (or if it was, not to the same extent). These new maps are fragile, delicate entities: they are connections that have the potential to become part of our hardwiring, yet they are also just one of many millions of new maps we create every day. To make a new map a part of our everyday lives, we need to give it some attention.[45]

The new maps generated when we have a dialogue using the CREATE model are often important to people's overall effectiveness at work and in life. They are about how to think better, how to function more efficiently. Ideas like "I need to listen to my hunches more" or "I need to prioritize better." You might compare these insights to patches for a computer program, or mini programs that can be drawn on for other uses later on.

My point is, the insights people have are potentially valuable resources. Like any other useful resource—such as a new tool a builder might purchase for removing nails—we should know a little about it so we know how else it might be useful, and make sure we put it somewhere we can find again easily. The way we do this mentally is by giving these new circuits enough attention.

As leaders our job is to give people's new maps attention and positive feedback, whatever has happened since they had their initial insight. If Joe comes back a week later and says "You know what, I did that spreadsheet and found it really useful," our focus should be on helping him deepen any new wiring he's developed. If he didn't get the spreadsheet completed, or even if he didn't do it at all, we still want to find ways to deepen any useful wiring that was created.[46]

The way we do this is described in the final big idea in this book: the FEELING model. FEELING stands for Facts, Emotions, Encouragement, Learning, Implications, and New Goals.

Facts

Emotions

Encourage

Learning

Implications

New

Goal

Figure 34, The FEELING model

FACTS

The first thing to do when following up about Joe's spreadsheet is simply to get the facts. Try to remain emotionally neutral in this phase and just get the information about what was done compared to what had been planned. Ask questions like "Did you get this completed exactly as you had planned?" Get people to be specific here. If Joe says, "I got it basically finished," ask for clarification: Find out what percentage of the spreadsheet he finished, as compared to his plans.

One up side to getting the facts is that people see what they've done, which is often more than they give themselves credit for.

If Joe hasn't done his spreadsheet, we still want to know the facts. However, because we're solutions-focused, we don't need to ask why he *didn't* do the task. It will be much more useful—to Joe, to you, and to what Joe learns out of this situation—to know the facts about what he *did* do. For example, how much thinking time did he put into the action, even if he didn't complete it? Or research time, or time spent discussing it with other people? In this situation, help the other person be as specific as possible, with questions like "How many minutes did you spend thinking about doing this?"

It's easy for us to go straight to "What got in the way?" yet this pathway rarely adds any value to anyone. Most adults don't need to be made wrong when they don't keep a promise; they do this well enough by themselves. What they need are dialogues that help them learn.

So the first part of the FEELING model is to get the facts, focusing on the facts of what can be observed: what was done, not what wasn't. Doing this takes a little awareness and practice; for many people it's a completely new habit.

EMOTIONS

Once you've got the facts about how far someone went with an action, the next step is to see how they *feel* about what they achieved. Notice we've had two steps so far, and still haven't asked for any details yet. Staying at a high level facilitates faster learning.

A useful question to ask here is "How do you feel about how you went with this project?" With Joe, it turns out he did the action completely, and was proud of his decision to go the extra mile. By distinguishing his emotions about what he did, you are giving the new circuits being created even more attention, in a whole other way. You are also harnessing the power of emotions, which are believed to be a key resource when it comes to creating long-term memory. We remember things we feel strongly about.

Another reason for checking on people's emotions early in the conversation is to address any strong emotions that might get in the way of useful conversations. For example, if Joe hadn't completed the spreadsheet he might feel guilty and frustrated, which would make it difficult to talk about what he'd learned. When people haven't completed an action they'd planned, help them put their emotions aside. You can do this by naming an emotion and having a conversation about it. With Joe you might let him know you're not going to make him wrong, and ask him not to be so tough on himself.

So the second part of the FEELING model is to check in on people's emotions. If they had a good experience completing their action, you deepen their wiring by focusing attention on these positive feelings. If they had a difficult time, you can help them put their emotions aside to allow a more useful conversation to follow.

ENCOURAGE

When you use the CREATE model, you're helping people think differently, and then getting them to do things they hadn't thought of immediately by themselves. Therefore you're stretching people, getting them to use different parts of their brain. Using a spreadsheet to make a complex decision might be obvious to you, but if someone had never done this, it might feel like a real challenge.

Given that people are being stretched here, it's important to encourage them generously, to help make the experience a positive one. You might acknowledge their efforts, appreciate what they had to do differently, or identify the challenges they faced and surmounted and validate these.

This is fairly obvious when people complete what they planned to. In this case remember to be specific with your acknowledgments—not just "Well done for stretching yourself" but "Well done for stretching yourself and thinking more deeply about this than you may have initially wanted to; I sense it took more effort than you initially wanted to give this." (There's more about encouraging people in "Accentuate the Positive" earlier in the book.)

Yet it's even more important to encourage others when they don't complete something. If Joe didn't get his spreadsheet done, find ways to encourage him anyway. If you give him grief instead, how will he feel next time you try to create new thinking around a different dilemma?

To encourage people who didn't achieve an action in full—or at all—focus on what they *did* do, not what they didn't. Find out about their thinking time, the energy they put into the action in other ways, and encourage them for this. Perhaps Joe didn't get his spreadsheet completed, but spent an hour on the way to work one day thinking through how he'd do it, which was more energy than he'd ever given before to a planning process. This is a big breakthrough, and celebrating it can help cement this new habit. Celebrating it means identifying it, naming it, acknowledging it. You could try a statement like "Good job going for such a big challenge this week! I know you meant to do it when you set it, and it's great that you put some solid thinking into it—that's a big leap from anything you've done in the past."

When you follow up, find ways to encourage people and you will be helping them turn their delicate new circuits into long-term habits.

We're going to go deeper into the concept of giving positive feedback in the next section of the book. For now I want to get across that encouragement and acknowledgment are essential when you follow up, and to focus on things that happened, not why things did not.

LEARNING

Finding out what people are learning is the central element of following up. We want to help identify any new wiring people are developing and new habits in the early stages of formation. And not just identify new wiring, but name it, understand it, hold it in our hands, see it from many angles. We want to give it lots of attention.

Again the questions can be simple, and it's better when they are.

With Joe you could ask, "What did you learn about yourself by doing this spreadsheet?"

It's tempting here to get lost in the details. Yet why ask about what was in Joe's spreadsheet when you can ask what he learned from completing it? What you most want to know is what he has learned about his own thinking, so ask that specifically. By focusing your attention on new habits rather than details, you're focusing other people's attention more sharply on these new circuits; you're watering one specific new seedling rather than spraying a hose over a whole garden.

If you can also give Joe a little encouragement for the new wiring he's developing, you'll be helping even more. Now you have given Joe's new maps attention and positive feedback together. In this way, you're not just watering that seedling, you're giving it nutrients too.

Questions you could ask to deepen people's learning include:

What was your big insight this week?
What did you find out about yourself?
What other insight did that then open up?
What did you discover about your thinking or habits?
What new habit did you notice starting to emerge?

Focus on the learning when you follow up. It's the best way to improve people's thinking.

IMPLICATIONS

Once you have the facts, checked in on emotions, encouraged them, and identified what the big learning was, next you want to explore the implications of what someone has learned. With Joe, he might have done the spreadsheet, be feeling really pleased with himself, and learned that it would be useful to step out of the details of his week more often and look at his schedule from a higher level. That's a pretty useful bit of learning—wouldn't it be great for Joe to make that a part of his working practices? So ask a question here like "What are the implications of this insight?"

Asking about the implications of what someone has learned means you are giving their new wiring even more attention, more focus, and making links to other parts of their brain. It's further embedding these new circuits.

Other questions you could ask to define the implications of what someone learned include:

What are the broader implications of being able to do this now?
Do you sense there could be other ways this new habit could be helpful?
What impact has this learning had on you?
Where else might this new skill be useful?
Can you see any other applications of what you've learned here?
How else might you use this kind of new thinking?

NEW GOAL

I am guessing you've worked out this final step. Joe had an insight out of a dialogue with you last week. He realized he needed to prioritize his projects. He had the idea of doing this on a spreadsheet as a better way to think. He went off and completed the spreadsheet. You followed up a few days later and found out he completed the action, was really pleased with himself, and learned it would be worth making this practice a regular part of his work.

What's emerged is a whole new dilemma around Joe being more organized. In a sense, this dilemma is a much more interesting one. It's something like: "I'd like to step above the details regularly but am worried this won't happen because I am so busy." Through a new round of the CREATE model, Joe might come up with an action to have a weekly "Step outside the box" session for thirty minutes with a colleague, to help each other prioritize their thinking more.

So the final part to the FEELING model is to identify the next goal to focus on.

Here's an example of the FEELING model in action, going back to Ellen and Sue at the magazine group. Sue wanted to get her sales going but thought everyone was in a slump. Through Ellen's help,

Sue became clear that getting her team inspired was her number one priority, but realized that she was all out of ideas after trying to inspire them for six months. At this point, Sue had an insight: As a result of seeing how much thinking she'd been doing, she saw that her people weren't doing much thinking about the targets at all. She realized they weren't on board with the targets. Sue decided to set up a meeting with everyone, and Ellen helped her plan the meeting in more detail while it was fresh in her mind, including setting deadlines and arranging to get help to make it a success.

Here's how the follow-up conversation between the two of them might then go, using the FEELING model.

Ellen: *So did you manage to get them together for the meeting—did you hit your target number of people there?* [Looking for the facts.]

Sue: *We had a better time than I'd expected. Twelve of them came along, it was great in the end.*

Ellen: *Congratulations, that's more than you'd hoped for, well done for pulling this off. How do you feel about yourself now?* [Asking about her feelings.]

Sue: *I'm really pleased with how it went. The meeting made a big difference, and now I feel like I am not pushing everyone so hard, they're more on board.*

Ellen: *Fantastic. Well, congratulations on getting the event together on such a short timeline . . . and for realizing that you needed to approach this differently, then for coming up with such a solid plan for the meeting, and for obviously winning on the day. Sounds like it was really worthwhile.* [Lots of acknowledgment.]

Sue: *Thanks!*

Ellen: *So do you mind if I ask* [A little permission there.]—*what is the big insight for you out of all this—what did you learn?*

Sue: *I guess it's that I don't need to push so hard. It's important that when I feel like I am struggling to stop and see how everyone else is doing.*

Ellen: *Sounds like a useful insight.* [Yet more acknowledgment.]

> *Do you mind if I ask something a bit more detailed . . . do you think this is an important insight, with implications for other projects you're working on? Have you noticed yourself doing anything different since you had this "aha"?*

Sue: *Actually I have . . . I think this whole idea has opened my mind to other people more, and I started to be more relaxed in my interviews with new people.*

Ellen: *Sounds like a new habit emerging there.*

Sue: *Definitely. And I'd like it to stay with me . . .*

Ellen: *Can I help at all?*

Sue: *Sure . . . I'd like to be more conscious of how others are feeling around me, but I get so tied up in my own thoughts . . .*

And right there you have the start of a new dilemma to work on, a more interesting *and* useful dilemma than the one we started from.

In summary, the final step to transforming performance is following up with people to help them recognize and therefore further embed the habits they are developing. By doing this in a positive and supportive way, we give people the encouragement they need to turn their delicate new circuits into full-blown hard wiring. It's not a difficult process, it takes just a few minutes—but it can make a world of difference.

■ ■ ■ ■ ■ ■ ■ **EXERCISE STATION FOR** ■ ■ ■ ■ ■ ■ ■

Follow Up

Find opportunities to practice this model. It needs to be after someone has decided to take on a challenging assignment of some sort, so a good way to do this is with a friend, so you can practice on each other. Help each other think through a dilemma, using all the models in the Six Steps, then make a time to follow up. Practice each of the elements above as you follow up—it might be helpful to have the book in front of you. Another great action is to create your own drawing or diagram of the FEELING model, to help you remember the elements.

_____

_____

_____

_____

_____

_____

_____

A SUMMARY OF THE SIX STEPS

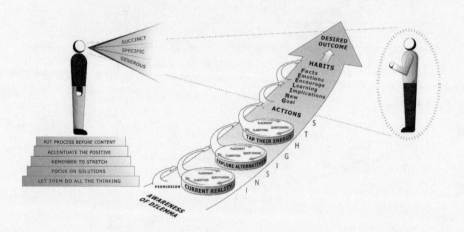

Figure 35, The Six Steps to Transforming Performance

The Six Steps to Transforming Performance are a new set of tools for improving people's thinking and dramatically improving their performance. These six steps are the core of being a Quiet Leader, and define a whole new way of communicating in the workplace.

The first step is to think about thinking; to let people do all the thinking, keep them focused on solutions, stretch their thinking, accentuate the positive, and follow good process. The second step is to listen for potential, and to not get too close. The third step is to speak with intent and to be succinct, specific, and generous. Step four is about the conversation: We dance toward insight by getting permission for harder conversations, placing people so they know where we're coming from, using thinking questions so that others do the thinking, and then clarifying their responses.

Once we know how to dance this way, in step five we create new thinking. We get people to become aware of their mental dilemmas and reflect more deeply on them by asking questions about their current reality. Once they have had an insight, we explore alternatives for how to move their insight into action, then we tap into the energy given off by the new connections being made.

Finally, we know that following up can make a big difference to the emergence of new wiring, so we focus on the facts and people's feelings. We encourage, listen for learning, look for implications, and then look for the next goal to focus on.

There have been two main themes running through the Six Steps. The first theme is how to have a conversation to resolve any type of dilemma. This covers the majority of interactions leaders have day to day with their people. The second theme is how you might use the various models inside the Six Steps more widely. For example, permission, placement, and clarifying can be very useful tools in many situations.

In the next section of the book we're going to turn things around a little. We're going to explore the most common activities that leaders engage in with their people, and see how the Six Steps can be applied, to help bring all of this even more to life for you.

Part Three

Putting the Six Steps to Use

Ideas are not enough.
They do not last.
Something practical must be done with them.

MARVIN BOWER,
FORMER MANAGING DIRECTOR OF MCKINSEY & COMPANY (2001)

When it comes to interacting with their people, you can break down the activities that leaders engage in into just a few categories: they create vision and strategy; they establish clear expectations; they help their people solve problems and make decisions; and finally they give performance feedback to promote learning and development.

The Six Steps to Transforming Performance can be applied to all of these activities in many different ways. In this section of the book we'll focus on three of the more challenging ones: how to help others solve problems; how to support people to make better decisions; and how to give feedback in various situations. I have also included a chapter on using the Six Steps with teams as well as an additional chapter on using these ideas with children. Following that is a guide to further resources, a glossary of terms, and lots of notes for reference.

USING THE SIX STEPS TO
HELP SOMEONE SOLVE A PROBLEM

*The greatest challenge to any thinker is stating
the problem in a way that will allow a solution.*

BERTRAND RUSSELL (1872–1970)

One of the more challenging interactions leaders have with their employees is when something isn't going right: a team needs to be replaced; a computer system isn't working; a launch isn't hitting its targets. It's when the employee has not been able to work out how to solve a problem and the leader is stepping in to help.

The standard leadership approach involves telling people what to do. The new way, the way of a Quiet Leader, is to improve people's thinking. Let's take a look at how this applies to solving problems.

Mark was a financial controller at a large technology company, in charge of the finances of the manufacturing division, the largest division in the business. Mark wanted to terminate the employment of Jeff, a long-term staff member, due to his poor performance over the last two years. The problem was, Mark was worried about how this could impact the morale of his team, many of whom held key roles. If it went down badly, the whole division's performance could suffer. Part of Mark's dilemma was that despite being a poor performer, Jeff was popular with everyone, and had been with the business for nearly twenty years.

Mark went to one of the people he reported to, Richard, who was in charge of finance at corporate headquarters. He shared his thoughts with Richard for a few minutes and clearly seemed stuck. He really did want to get rid of Jeff, but also saw that this could have big repercussions.

If Richard was like many senior executives, he might ask Mark lots of questions to get an idea of what the situation was about, and then make some suggestions. Given that Mark was a strong-willed individual, any suggestion that Richard made would be heavily debated, so the conversation might take several hours. In the end, Mark would not be likely to leave with much clarity.

However, if Richard had mastered the Six Steps, the conversation could take just ten minutes. Instead of Mark leaving uncertain about what to do next, he would leave the dialogue clear about what needed to happen and energized about taking action, and then quickly resolve the problem. Here's how the central part of such a dialogue between them might go.

Mark: *I've got this senior guy, he's been here for years, but he's just not performing anymore. I can tell his heart's not in the work any longer. His work's been steadily declining for a few years now. The problem is, he's really central to the team—everyone likes him, he organizes the social events, all that kind of thing. I'm worried that replacing him might have a big impact on the morale of the group. They're a very tight team.*

Richard: *I appreciate you bringing your concerns to me. Do you want to throw around a few ideas about this?* [Getting permission.]

Mark: *Yeah, I could do with all the help I can get. What do you think I should do here?* [People often start a conversation wanting you to provide the answers. It doesn't mean you should!]

Richard: *I'd like to ask a few questions and see if I can help you organize your thoughts here, rather than tell you what I think you should do. If we can't see anything useful this way, of course I will let you know what I think as well. There are a lot of po-*

tential problems that could happen here, but I want to focus more on solutions. Is that okay with you? [Very thorough placement here, to be sure the other person knows exactly what's going to happen.]

Mark: *Are you saying you don't want to know any details?*

Richard: *It might sound strange but the less detail I know, the more I may be able to help you. Let me see if I can simplify this a little, I want to see if I have got your challenge . . . You want to fire Jeff but are worried about the impact on people. Is that right?* [Getting the dilemma.]

Mark: *Well, maybe I'm not really sure if firing him is the right thing to do right now . . .*

Richard: *So how can I best help you here—where would you like to focus, on whether or not to fire Jeff, or whether to take another approach, or on how to manage the impact on the team? Which is the key issue right now to focus on?*

Notice that we're still trying to get to the central dilemma, through using permission, placement, questioning, and clarifying. Defining the central dilemma before you go deeper will save time and energy. Not doing this is one of the reasons conversations go in circles. I am keeping this part of the dialogue short here so that the book doesn't become five hundred pages, but in real life this could go on for a while.

Mark: *As you were talking to me I think I may have got a bit of clarity . . . I really have made the decision to fire him, I'm just avoiding doing it because I know what might happen—it's going to be painful and it could be a bit of a drama. Some of my team came up to me last week and said so.*

Richard: *So what you're saying is, you need to fire Jeff, but want to work out how to do this with minimal pain for everyone?*

Mark: *Yeah, I guess that's it. If I was really honest with myself, I know it has to happen, but I keep putting it off.* [Now we have the main dilemma.]

Richard: *Are you interested in talking about this further, then?* [Getting permission again as this is a new conversation.]

Mark: *Sure.*

Richard: *So you want to fire Jeff but want to do so with minimal pain for everyone.* [Placement again, to make sure they both stay very focused on the central dilemma.] *How long have you been thinking about this?* [Here is the classic thinking question, to help Mark start to see his own thinking.]

Mark: *I don't know, maybe . . . hmm . . .* [Mark takes a moment to reflect and think more deeply. He's moved into the reflection phase of the four faces of insight; his eyes are probably looking up.] *I guess it's been on my mind for a couple of months now, it comes and goes, but it's almost always there in the background . . . though I've known he's had to go for over a year.*

Richard: *So this thought has been around quite intensely for a few months.* [Clarifying.]

Mark: *Yeah, I guess it has.*

Richard: *So how important is it that you get him off the team, on a scale of one to ten, where ten is critical?*

Mark: *You know what, now that I think about it, it's probably a seven out of ten. It's not a ten or I would have handled this already.*

Richard: *So you know it's important to do this, but not that important that it can't be put off.*

Mark: *Yep . . . that's true, I guess.*

Richard: *How do you feel when you think about putting this off more?*

Now you might think that Richard has an agenda behind the way he asked that last question, and if he said it a certain way that might be true. Yet all he's asked is "What impact does this thought have on you?" He's just helping Mark see his own thinking more clearly.

Mark: *I'd never thought about that . . . that's a good question . . . you know what, I think putting this off is draining my en-*

ergy. I hadn't really noticed this . . . it's time I got this re-solved. [Mark has just made new connections in a flash—he's moved into the illumination phase of the four faces of insight. Now we're wrapping up the current reality phase of the questions and moving into exploring alternatives.]

Richard: *Sounds like you got some clarity here. Would it be worth talking a bit more about this? Do you know what you need to do next?* [This is a form of permission as we move between the phases.]

Mark: *Look, I have a general sense of what I need to do, it's just forming now. I'm going to work with a few of my people before I tell everyone and get some buy-in individually to make this less of a drama.*

Richard: *Sounds like a great idea. Do you want to flesh out some different ways you might do this, a few different options?* [This is the exploring alternatives question.]

Mark: *Yeah, I was going to set up a meeting but I guess it might be useful to think this through a bit.*

Richard: *So you want to work out how to get buy-in from a few people about Jeff.* [He's moving on to placement, this time about the new conversation to explore alternatives.] *How can I best help you think this through—do you want to throw out a few options and flesh out some ideas here, or maybe talk to some other people to get a few ideas, or do some reading on this? What's going to work for you?* [Now he's asking the exploring alternatives questions, staying out of the detail of the options.]

Mark: *I think I know what I need . . . I just need to book a lunch meeting with three people, and do it now. In fact, I'm going to make some calls right after this.* [Through exploring options Mark has got clarity about what he needs to do; he was ready to jump in and make a decision.]

Richard: *Great. Do you want me to support you in any way on this?* [Tap their energy question.]

Mark: *No, you've been helpful, thanks so much for your input here.*

Richard: *Great. So has this been useful?*

Mark: *Absolutely, thanks very much. I've just lifted a cloud that's been hanging around for a year.*

In this case there was nothing to do in the tap their energy phase. The conversation could just as easily have gone down the path of spending a few minutes exploring how he wanted to run the one-on-one meetings with his people, around when to schedule them, or asking if he wanted to set a deadline for when he would get these done by. Sometimes you'll only use one or two parts of the CREATE model, and people don't need any more help.

Let's summarize this scenario. Mark came to Richard with a problem, wanting some advice. Richard could easily have given him advice, such as to speak to his team directly. In this instance Mark would probably argue with this idea because he hadn't made the connections himself. Richard might suggest Mark do a 360-degree feedback on the team and try to get Jeff to leave of his own accord. This would be debated. He might then suggest that Mark consider the competency profiles of Jeff's job, and see if there's a chance to have a formal performance review, and attempt to get Jeff to decide it was time to go.

Richard could have given Mark lots of different advice; yet in this instance he didn't suggest Mark do anything at all. All he did was help Mark think through the issue on the table more clearly, more objectively, and make connections for himself. All of this was fast, energizing, and amazingly simple. And the result was Mark went off and handled the problem quickly.

Would Mark have come to this decision on his own? Quite likely yes, but remember the issue has been sitting around for two years already, and might have sat there a lot longer. Had Mark let the situation fester it may have become a real problem, resulting in having to fire Jeff in a negative way. Instead of this, through Richard's quiet leadership, Mark made some hard decisions sooner, with everyone better off as a result.

Let's explore some other types of problems, and how the Six Steps could be applied to each. Rather than giving you complete dialogues,

I'll give you some questions you might ask for each dilemma, to help illustrate the patterns in the process. I won't cover the common questions you start a dialogue with, but focus instead on the more useful questions that could help.

Dilemma: I need to be more organized but I'm overwhelmed by how much is going on.

"How committed are you to resolving this immediately?"

"How do you feel about the amount of thinking you've given to this challenge so far?"

"Do you have a clear vision of the level of organization you'd like to achieve?"

"Exactly how clear is this vision, on a scale of one to ten?"

"How clear are you about what you need to do to get organized, on a scale of one to ten?"

"How can I best help you think this through further?"

Dilemma: I have to replace a staff member but can't work out who we need.

"How important is this as a priority right now?"

"How do you feel about the amount of thinking you've given this so far?"

"How do you feel about the quality of the thinking you've given this so far?"

"What resources do you need, to help you think this through better?"

"Which part of the challenge is most holding you back?"

"What do you sense is the next step?"

Dilemma: I need to get our costs down but can't find cuts anywhere.

"How important is this to you?"

"How important is this to the organization?"

"How do you feel about the amount of attention you've given this so far?"

"What types of processes have worked for you in the past to solve a challenge like this?"

"How do you feel about how you are tackling this project overall—organized, chaotic, disciplined?"

"What do you sense might be the missing link here?"

In summary, the Six Steps to Transforming Performance are very useful for helping people solve problems. Just define an issue as a dilemma, and then follow the process. Using the Six Steps to solve problems can help you resolve problems in minutes instead of hours. Suddenly you could find yourself with spare time and not know what to do with it. Now *there's* a more interesting dilemma to have to resolve.

USING THE SIX STEPS
TO HELP SOMEONE MAKE A DECISION

*The real dividing line between the things we call work and the
things we call leisure is that in leisure, however active we may be,
we make our own choices and our own decisions.
We feel for the time being that our life is our own.*

ANONYMOUS

We've seen how useful the Six Steps can be around solving a problem. They can be just as useful when helping someone make a decision. Let's explore this with a new case study, and then I will give you other useful questions to use in this arena.

Rebecca was a director of Human Resources at a midsized investment bank. She was having trouble deciding between two hires for a new senior role. The position involved managing the learning programs for hundreds of highly intelligent people. She'd narrowed her candidates down to two: one seemed to have stronger people skills, the other more experience. They were both ideal for the role and Rebecca couldn't decide whom to choose. She brought this up at a monthly meeting with her CEO, Robert.

If Robert wasn't drawing on the ideas in this book, he might try guessing at different mental frames Rebecca could try on, like telling her to trust her gut, or to check the data carefully. These would not be bad suggestions per se, just unlikely to be useful.

Or Robert might try to make the decision for her, by asking questions about the candidates and then making his recommendation. However, even if he makes a great decision, at senior levels in organizations, this undermines people's credibility and their self-confidence. Better to improve Rebecca's ability to make difficult decisions on her own.

As a Quiet Leader, Robert's first step is to identify the central dilemma in as few words as possible. In this case, through quick questioning, the central dilemma became "I just want to hire the absolute best of the two but am worried about how to do this."

Robert would then use the Dance of Insight model to ask thinking questions. In this instance he helped Rebecca come to her own insight in only five questions. Here's an outline of what happened.

Question 1. How do you feel about the amount of thinking you've given this so far?
The answer was "exhausted." She'd spent weeks grappling with this.

Question 2. How important is it that you come to an answer quickly?
The answer was "100 percent." She needed to decide in the next twenty-four hours, but was feeling completely stuck.

Question 3. How clear are you about which part of your thinking needs to be broken down more?
Her answer, after a few moments' reflection, was that she needed to focus on getting her team to support this, even though she had to make the final decision.

Question 4. How clear are you on a scale of one to ten about how to get your team involved in making the decision?
Her answer was a "six," but the actual number isn't what was so helpful here. What helped was getting Rebecca to think very

deeply, which in this instance involved stepping through the following ideas over a few seconds:

- How she'd got her team involved in decisions in the past
- What had worked when she'd got her team involved in other decisions
- How she was feeling about getting them involved using similar approaches this time

It was the sum of these rapid connections that brought Rebecca closer to her big aha.

Question 5. How can I help you close the gap and get to a "ten"?
At this point Rebecca had her big insight. She'd come unstuck rushing her team into a decision before, and this one needed to happen in twenty-four hours. Her big insight was realizing that fear of this happening again was freezing up her thinking.

Once Rebecca saw her own thinking clearly, it became obvious what she needed to do: instead of starting a torrent of emails bouncing between people, she needed to make some old-fashioned telephone calls to discuss this with her people in real time. In the end it took being willing to get up early one morning, but in an hour of calls the decision was made, and everyone felt involved.

All Robert did here was help Rebecca notice her own thought processes. As a result, she was able to resolve her own dilemma and make her decision. The next time she noticed she'd stopped thinking clearly, she'd probably use this mental muscle again—to step back and noticing her own thinking processes. Her thinking had improved.

Other useful questions to help people make decisions

"How long have you been thinking about this decision?"

"Do you have a process you normally use for making big decisions?"

"How do you feel about the amount of thinking you've done on this so far?"

"Which part of this decision is the central issue?"

"How important is this decision, on a scale of one to ten?"

"Do you have a timetable for this decision?"

"How close to making the decision do you feel you are?"

"Do you know what you need to do to make this decision?"

"What parameters are you using to make this decision?"

"What would be a great process for making the decision, versus the decision itself?"

"How could I best help you decide here?"

When using the Six Steps to help people make decisions, let the other person drive the thinking. It's not that different from using the models for solving a problem. Let's explore two other models to keep in mind around improving decisions.

MAKING DECISIONS WITH THE CLARITY OF DISTANCE

Sometimes the person charged with making big decisions is the least appropriate person to make them. They're too close: the volume of details they have in mind stops them from seeing the patterns, or their own filters or agendas inhibit them from processing information accurately. Rebecca, for example, had a hot spot about rushing her team to a decision. Her internal electrical signals were taking up the capacity her neurons should have been using to analyze the issues and make new connections.

What helps here is identifying which of the elements of the Clarity of Distance model are getting in the way. If Rebecca had been stopped by a filter rather than a hot spot, for example to hire one of the potentials because of their cultural background, she'd be able to think more clearly just by identifying this filter.

Additional questions to help people make decisions using the Clarity of Distance model include:

"How clear is your thinking here?"

"Which part of this decision is the hardest to process?"

"What would make this decision much easier?"

"What do you personally need to be able to make this decision easily?"

Once we've identified what's getting in the way of good thinking, we can develop strategies to ensure that a more balanced decision is made. As leaders we can pose suggestions once people have had an insight about what's inhibiting their thinking. Strategies that might improve decision making include:

- Getting many other people's perspectives
- Using a logical, well-structured decision process such as developing ratings for different qualities
- Taking a walk. According to neuroscientist John Ratey, any kind of physical activity helps the brain process ideas.[1]
- Have a lie-down. I know this doesn't sound very practical, but a recent study showed people came up with better ideas while horizontal![2]

MAKING DECISIONS WITH THE CHOOSE YOUR FOCUS MODEL

Many people launch into projects without spending enough time defining their objectives, or enough time planning.

Introducing the Choose Your Focus model into conversations reminds people to start at the top with their thinking. It's especially helpful when people are lost in the details. Some questions you could ask include:

"What's your overall goal?"

"What's your vision of the perfect outcome?"

"Do you know where you're trying to get to?"

"Are you clear about your plan for achieving this goal?"

"How well fleshed out is your plan?"

"Would it be worth spending more time on vision or planning?"

In summary, making decisions can be a difficult process, and having a sounding board can make a big difference. Especially if that person can help you improve the process by which decisions are made. The Six Steps are an excellent tool to help.

USING THE SIX STEPS TO GIVE FEEDBACK

*Enthusiasm and loving encouragement
establish and cultivate new synapses.*

THOMAS B. CZERNER (2001)

Feedback is the delicate art of letting people know the score. Feedback gives people information that helps them learn and grow.

Giving feedback is central to good leadership. It's something leaders can do hourly, daily, weekly, monthly, quarterly, annually, or over any number of years. Giving feedback is also one of the more difficult conversations leaders must have, one with the most potential for things to go wrong. A survey in 2003 by an Australian business school found "coaching staff" in the top five management challenges, just after "keeping cool under pressure."[3] Partly as a result of this, many leaders give detailed feedback only once a year.[4]

The Six Steps in this book can be applied to almost all feedback situations at work, the exception being late-stage performance management when a warning needs to be given. In this case there's usually too much emotional charge on both sides for a productive two-way conversation to occur. Let's focus here on three common types of feedback situations: giving feedback for great performance, below-par performance, and poor performance.

GIVING FEEDBACK FOR GREAT PERFORMANCE

Most people love receiving positive feedback. It makes us stand a little taller and feel like the world is a great place; it can even be the
highlight of a whole year. Given how good it feels, and the fact that
it's legal, ethical, and has no unintended side effects, you'd think people would naturally do lots of it at work. Yet this is far from the case.
A 2004 Gallup survey found 65 percent of US workers received no
recognition at all in the workplace in the last year.[5]

Any organization that wants to improve its people's performance
could do well just by making sure there is enough positive feedback
flowing between their employees. Without positive feedback, we literally don't know how we are doing and can't perform to our best.
Another Gallup survey of four million people found that people who
received regular recognition and praise increased their individual
productivity, increased engagement amongst their colleagues, and
were more likely to stay with the organization.[6]

Here's a crazy idea: It's widely accepted that workers need down-
time to perform at their best, so governments in most developed na-
tions have legislated that workers are entitled to several weeks of
vacation each year. Maybe it's time they legislated that workers get
sufficient positive feedback each year, too.

Let's explore some of the main issues to keep in mind when giving positive feedback. Then I'll flesh out a new approach to giving
positive feedback that takes advantage of opportunities to improve
people's thinking.

Be specific

There is a big difference between saying "You did great" and
"You did great getting that meeting together in such little time
and with almost no resources." If we want our impact to be the
same as our intent, it's important to be as specific as possible
when delivering positive feedback. This sometimes means thinking a
bit more deeply, taking more care with your feedback, reflecting
more.

Let's say a colleague produces an excellent report and you want to be more specific in your feedback. The kinds of questions you could consider include:

- What was great about the report?
- What effort did they need to put in?
- What challenges did they face in completing this?
- How does the report impact you or others?
- What did they do that made a difference?

Be generous

Few people are comfortable receiving positive feedback. So when giving it, try to speak in a way that allows the other person to take what you're saying on board. Choose your words carefully so you don't sound insincere, or you could do more harm than good. Take the time to reflect. Think about how to get across your feedback so that people will seriously consider what you're saying.

Use permission and placement

When people hear they're going to get some feedback they automatically fear the worst. So it's useful to ask permission to give someone some feedback before launching into it; letting people know what to expect can be helpful too. A simple statement like "I have some positive feedback about how you did on that project—it's all good news, is now a good time to share this with you?" Even when giving positive feedback, some permission and placement can help. Most people don't feel comfortable accepting positive feedback, so it might help to say "I know you're going to try to brush this off, but I want you to really consider what I am going to say here. . . ."

Strive for self-directed learning

Allowing people to give themselves positive feedback will help them make connections in their own mind. You could do this either before or after you give your own feedback. Use the Dance of Insight model to help someone identify what he or she did well. This is a great way to get people to become more self-aware, and a lot of fun too. Questions you could ask here include:

"Tell me six things you did really well."

"Tell me three things you learned about yourself here."

"Tell me about two big challenges you faced and overcame."

"Tell me what resources you had to find, internally and externally, to get this done."

A new approach to giving positive feedback that goes a little further

When someone has done a great job, you are faced with a great opportunity to identify new wiring they've developed, and to give this wiring enough attention to help it become a part of who they are. Doing this when someone is feeling good is obviously easier than when they have under-performed. Yet our common approach to giving feedback is only to interact in any detail when things have gone wrong. I call this the "why bother talking about the good stuff?" phenomenon. It's like a baseball player who only hits the ball when the bases are loaded, and takes every other pitch.

Let's make this more tangible with a dialogue. Rather than put notes after the dialogue, here's an opportunity to deepen your connections with an exercise. As you read through the dialogue, note the models you see and write them down around the text.

Manager: *I'd like to take a few minutes to talk about the great job you did with hiring those new people. Don't panic—it's all good news. Is now okay for you?*

Direct report: *Sure.*

Manager: *I think you did a fantastic job hiring those people and wanted to tell you what I noticed . . . I didn't know how you would get quality people into those positions within such a tight deadline, and I want you to know your commitment and focus really shone through. You didn't give up when everyone said it couldn't be done. Also your leadership came through in the way you got a whole team to support you, and your creativity stood out in the way you got everyone to come up with a lot of different ideas. People tell me you're having a positive impact across the department and I just wanted to acknowledge you for such great work.*

What would it be like if every manager in your organization regularly gave feedback like that, when it was deserved? What difference would it make to people's morale, commitment, and dedication? This is an example of great positive feedback, and it's also where we tend to stop. Yet much more is possible. Take a look at what else could happen:

Direct report: *Wow—thanks so much for the great feedback . . . I had no idea of the impact I was having outside of my small team.*

Manager: *Well, you have been making an impact, and you might be interested to know several people told me, without my asking, what a great job you've been doing. Would you like to give yourself some feedback here as to how you think you did as well?*

Direct report: *Sure . . . I guess. I don't like to talk about myself, though.*

Manager: *Would you be willing to give it a shot?*

Direct report: *Sure. I guess I was anxious taking on the project with the tight deadline but I decided to give it one hundred percent. I'm just glad it went well, not to say a little relieved, too.*

Manager: *Do you mind if I ask you a couple of questions to help you identify what you learned here?*

Direct report: *Sure.*

Manager: *What new skills or muscles do you think you developed in taking on this project, what did you learn about yourself?*

Direct report: *I think I learned the importance of asking for help, and the power of getting a team behind you. I couldn't have done this on my own. I went to a colleague and we worked through a few ideas and I realized then the difference it would make to get the team behind me. Normally I would try and go this alone but in this case I tried a new approach . . .*

Manager: *Is this a habit you would like to develop? Would you like me to support you in building this new mental muscle?*

Direct report: *You know . . . that would be great—I would really appreciate that . . . though don't be too tough on me if I forget!*

Manager: *I promise to only interact about this in a positive way—I won't jump on you when you don't do this. Maybe you should tell me what might work for you—how could I best help you turn this into a habit?*

Direct report: *If you could just ask me about it gently in our weekly meeting . . . that would be great.*

Manager: *It's a deal. Thanks for your honesty, and your willingness to let me stretch you a little. I appreciate being able to work with you on this level. Thanks.*

The approach above is obviously different from how a lot of feedback is given in the workplace. It's the approach of the Quiet Leader. It's an approach that the company in Singapore, which I opened the book with, could do well to train its managers in, instead of having them stand over people's shoulders telling them what to do.

People thrive on positive feedback.[7] Daniel Goleman, in his book *Emotional Intelligence*,[8] found that social isolation was roughly twice as detrimental to our health as smoking. The opposite of social isolation is social connectedness, and what better way to be connected than to get regular direct feedback about the impact you have on others? Giving and receiving this kind of positive feedback might take a little getting used to, and it might take getting over our paranoia about other people's agendas, but I think it's worth the trouble.

To finish my thoughts on positive feedback, here's a story from another event in Singapore. I was finishing a keynote on "Reinventing the Manager" and was talking about the importance of positive feedback. At the end of the talk a woman stood up confidently and said, "This all sounds great but it definitely won't work here—

positive feedback is just not in our culture." Many people nodded in agreement. I reflected for a moment about how to respond, then asked people who had children to stand up. About two thirds of the room stood up. "Now think of a time when your kids were young and they did something for the first time, like walking, or saying a new word. Can you all picture something?" Everyone standing nodded in agreement. "Now sit down if you automatically gave your child positive feedback in that moment." And everyone sat down. The first woman jumped back up again, her face now shining with the energy of an illumination. "So you're saying that we have the wiring we need to give positive feedback, we're just not in the habit of using it at work."

■ ■ ■ ■ ■ ■ ■ **EXERCISE STATION FOR** ■ ■ ■ ■ ■ ■ ■ ■

Giving Feedback for Great Performance

I have given this exercise to hundreds of managers over the years and heard it has changed the culture of many teams very quickly. The exercise is to give positive feedback once a day for a whole week, practicing being succinct, specific, and generous. Then make some notes about the impact this has on you and your team at the end of the week, being as specific as possible with your notes.

_____

_____

_____

_____

_____

_____

GIVING FEEDBACK FOR BELOW-PAR PERFORMANCE

Giving positive feedback when someone has done well is obviously a good idea and seems fairly straightforward. Dealing with someone who hasn't performed at their best can be a bit more complex.

Our first response to underperformance is usually to tell people what they did wrong. However, in a study I mentioned briefly earlier on, it was found that employees reacted negatively to criticism more than half the time and reacted positively to criticism just once out of thirteen times. In other words, the most likely response to criticism will be a negative one, the next most likely response is no impact, and the chance that criticism will be helpful is about once every three weeks if you dished it out every workday.

When we haven't performed well, we feel defensive, guilty, upset, frustrated, angry, or any combination of these. Trying to pinpoint the cause of the problem heightens these emotions, which isn't helpful to anyone. We're all masters of self-criticism and don't need a lot of assistance in this area.

As we learned in the chapter "It's Practically Impossible to Deconstruct Our Wiring," when we focus on what went wrong and why, we might find lots of reasons for failure, but finding these is unlikely to move us toward future success. And bear in mind that we are deepening the circuits that caused us to fail in the first place. Understanding the cause of failure is very helpful for managing processes, but when managing people we need a different approach.

When people underperform, rather than give them negative feedback or work out what went wrong, use the Six Steps to help them have insights for themselves. Letting people come to their own insights when things haven't gone well is more comfortable for everyone, and is more likely to deliver the outcome everyone wants: learning and behavior change for next time.

Alison is a marketing manager for an alcohol marketing company. She's done okay at one of her major annual projects, a big marketing event for a core brand, but her boss Enrico feels she could have done better compared to other years. He's scheduled a one-on-one conversation wisely: early in the week before she gets mentally tired, mid-morning while she has energy, and at a quiet cafe where they'll be free to talk openly. You might like to write down the models that Enrico is using here.

Enrico: *Thanks for taking the time to talk this through. I sense from how you responded to my request that you're probably not comfortable talking about this, so I appreciate you taking the time to do so anyway.*

Alison: *That's okay, I'm not happy about what happened but it's better we talk than let it hang around, I guess.*

Enrico: *Quite possibly. First I want to clarify that you're okay to have this conversation now, it's something fairly personal. Are you in a reasonable frame of mind to do this now?*

Alison: *Sure.*

Enrico: *Great, thanks. Also I want to check that you have forty-five minutes, and ask that we both switch off our phones so we don't get distracted.*

Alison: *No problem.*

Enrico: *Thanks. I want you to know there's nothing to be overly concerned about, your job's not in jeopardy, and more important, I am not here to get on your case about what happened. In fact, I am not going to talk about what happened much at all. What I'd like to do is see how I can best help you fulfill your potential in your role, if that's something you're interested in.*

Alison: *I appreciate you letting me know about that up front. I wasn't sure what to expect . . . I've been pretty down on myself about the event for a week already.*

So far all that's happened is lots of permission and placement. Enrico is putting process before content, planning for the success of the conversation itself. The conversation has taken two minutes so far, which might feel like a waste of time; however, without enough permission and placement, Alison is likely to feel defensive, and as a result they could easily go on much longer sidetracks. As a rule, the more potential there is for things to go wrong, the more time you should spend establishing permission and placing people.

Enrico: *Great. All I want to do is help you do your best job. I am aware that you haven't done as well as you have in the past, but I am not here to give you a hard time in any way—the event is past and I am here to help you move forward. To start with I want you to have the opportunity to give yourself some feedback about the event, to rate yourself and your performance. Tell me, on a scale of one to ten, how well do think you did at this project?*

Enrico is getting into the details about the event, not just Alison's thinking, but he's using metrics to keep the conversation at a high level. This helps keep the focus on learning rather than details. If he asked "How do you think it went?" she might interpret this as a request to describe all the problems. Remember, it's a slippery slope to the problem.

Alison: *I guess I delivered about six out of ten . . .*
Enrico: *So a little over half of what you're capable of.*
Alison: *Yeah, I was not very happy with myself at all.*
Enrico: *I appreciate your honesty here . . . so without getting into all the problems that happened, could you tell me what you learned from the exercise?*
Alison: *I guess I haven't worked that out yet—mostly I've just been annoyed with myself.*
Enrico: *Would you be willing to have that conversation with me now?*
Alison: *I think I expected it to go like other events and be easy, and when it wasn't I tried to do it all by myself. I didn't want anyone to know it wasn't going well, maybe to kinda save face . . . so I didn't ask for help.*
Enrico: *That would certainly make it harder, especially since the event is a real team project. Is that something you would be willing to talk about with me a bit more? It's something pretty personal.*
Alison: *Sure. It's on the table now.*
Enrico: *My question is a simple one. How can I best support you to*

turn this insight into a habit? How can I help you hardwire what you've learned about yourself here? Is that something you're interested in first of all?

Alison: *Absolutely. The last few weeks were hell and I am beginning to see it was partly self-imposed. So, yes. I guess what would help is just asking me about this at our weekly meetings, reminding me, kind of asking me how I am going with asking for help. I hate doing it, but if I don't sort this out now I probably never will.*

The conversation wraps up here with Enrico agreeing to follow up weekly with Alison about asking for help, for six weeks. Then they spend the balance of their scheduled time getting to know each other better, including discussing Alison's goals for her career, something they had not done so far.

During this ten minute conversation Alison put aside her exhausting guilt, and uncovered a habit that was a big reason she did not succeed. During the process she also developed more rapport and trust with her boss. Alison will probably never forget this project, this lesson, and of course, this manager. Enrico has helped her performance improve, without any specific suggestions, ideas, content, or advice. All he did was leave his agenda out of this, stay out of the details, let her do the thinking, focus on solutions, and help her turn her insights into habits.

GIVING FEEDBACK FOR POOR PERFORMANCE

Francesco is a manager in a large insurance company. One of his direct team, Andrew, has done a six-figure deal with a supplier that he shouldn't have done without getting Francesco's sign-off, according to protocols.

Interacting with poor performance is similar to dealing with performance that's just below par. The main difference is the amount of emotional charge both parties may experience. Francesco could confront Andrew and tell him he's done wrong. The reason for doing that would be to make sure it doesn't happen again. Yet because they are both quite headstrong men, confronting Andrew directly is likely to result in a lot of emotional tension. While Andrew might remember not to do it again, he won't have learned anything useful about himself, and the relationship between them will have gone downhill.

Bear in mind that the amount of emotional charge here means that Andrew might feel attacked if all Francesco said was "what happened?" So to interact in a way that won't flare into an argument, Francesco needs to first deal directly with the fact that this is a difficult conversation: the conversation won't go well without a lot of establishing permission and a lot of placement. It pays to be strategic about when to have the discussion, choosing a time when Andrew is less likely to be reactive, such as on a Friday evening over drinks.

Once the conversation has been set up well, Francesco needs to diffuse the strong emotional charge that comes with poor performance. It's difficult to have conversations about learning or solutions with guilt, self-flagellation, frustration, fear, sadness, or anger just below the surface.

Once the right environment has been set up, Francesco would establish permission, use a lot of placement, and take steps to put aside any strong emotions. Then the rest of the conversation is not that different to any other situation using this model. The hard work is all up front.

Some of the questions that Francesco might ask:

"How can we talk about this in a solutions-focused way?"
"How can this conversation be the most useful to you?"
"What's the big insight you've had from what's happened?"
"What have you learned from this whole situation?"

When it comes to dealing with underperformance, if our commitment is to people's learning, the more emotional charge there might be, the more essential it is to use a self-directed approach. This takes a willingness to put aside your own emotional response to a situation and focus on how to make the feedback experience of maximum value to the other person.

In summary, if our goal as leaders is to improve people's performance, then lots of feedback is essential, whatever has happened. Without feedback, we can't learn. However, we need to move away from the current paradigm of constructive performance feedback, a nice way of saying "politely tell people what they did wrong!" In its place, respectfully ask people what they learned, and how you can best help them to improve even further. To be more specific, when people do well, give them lots of positive feedback, be specific about it, and find ways to deepen any new habits emerging from their successes. When people underperform, venting your emotions as a leader is unlikely to do anything to improve their performance. The best way to make a difference is to let them do the thinking and be there to help them learn everything they can about themselves from the situation. This approach will build trust and respect, and make people want to do well. It will improve people's thinking, and over time, transform their performance.

USING THE SIX STEPS WITH TEAMS

You develop a team to achieve what one person cannot accomplish alone. All of us alone are weaker, by far, than if all of us are together.

MIKE KRZYZEWSKI, DUKE UNIVERSITY BASKETBALL COACH (2001)

I was walking in the park with my daughter recently when I ran into a new neighbor with his own little girl in tow. We talked about our respective professions while pushing the girls on the swings. His name was Antoine and he worked as a cable TV journalist. Antoine loved to write, but he'd just been promoted to a management role and was now in charge of a team of writers and camera operators. "It's like having a football team to coach," he said, shaking his head. "Except one person has no arms, one is scared of the ball, another can't run at all, and the others just don't want to be on the team anymore. How do you work with people like that?" he asked, throwing his hands in the air.

Antoine is far from alone in this challenge. Making the leap from content expert to manager is a critical step in every leader's development, and it's often not an easy one. The Six Steps can be a big help at this juncture. These steps provide a map for how to improve the performance of a team by improving the way the team thinks.

Without an effective team leader, team-think can be very inefficient. Time gets wasted on long, unnecessary conversations that don't add value to anyone. As a result, the best contributors may opt out of participating fully. If a team leader can stay out of the details, keep the group focused on solutions, and help them structure their thinking, they can really improve how the team communicates and therefore how they perform.

When the way a group thinks is well managed, the thinking is like parallel processing: the way two computer chips work twice as fast by working together, each doing a different part of the process. Let's explore in more detail how some of the models in this book are relevant to teams.

Let them do all the thinking

The role of a team leader is to facilitate the team's thinking, to help them think more productively and effectively than they would without the leader. However, it has to be the team doing the thinking, not the leader. Ignore this principle and people might humor you for a while, but ultimately you'll generate friction rather than synergy. As the leader you want to harness the team's collective thinking ability, rather than try to convince them of your ideas. Establish permission, do lots of placement and ask thinking questions. Above all, stay out of the details and problems. The CREATE model is also a great way of organizing the group's thought processes. Get the group to focus on the current reality of any situation first—what is known, what the facts are—before exploring alternatives widely, then tap the energy of the group, leveraging the expertise and motivations of individual players.

Focus on solutions

If you had a retention challenge, a team could spend a day dissecting the problem, or a day working out what to do about it. I've noticed that teams naturally prefer to focus on the problems. Discussing problems requires less commitment than discussing solutions, and in teams where people don't want to take ownership for things, it's going to be more comfortable for everyone if they focus on problems.

As a leader, your job is to gently steer the team toward a more useful direction, solutions, and then let them do the thinking. The Choose Your Focus model can be helpful here. Talk about it, or even put it up on a whiteboard to keep alive the idea of not getting lost in details, problem, or drama during a meeting. There's more on this coming up.

Give positive feedback

Teams need positive feedback as much as individuals, possibly even more. When people get together their emotions get amplified. It's like when shallow waves at the beach join together, there is a rush of water upward as the peak of each wave adds to the other. A little positive feedback can have a big impact as it bounces around between members of the team.

Create opportunities for positive feedback by establishing clear expectations on every level, so that everyone knows the game that's being played. Clear expectations start with having well-defined goals. It's also important to define how the team will work together, exploring things like operating policies and standards, the "rules of engagement." The team itself can generate these, with guidance from the leader. The more explicit the game and the rules are, the easier it is for everyone to participate fully, and the easier it is to give positive feedback when people do well.

Make them stretch

Most of us have had experiences of being on a team with a big mission to accomplish, with a goal that's a bit of a stretch. It's often during an emergency, like when a family has to work together to deal with a blackout. In wartime, soldiers experience a level of teamwork they may never again experience; many miss the experience and the bonding that results.

Helping teams set stretch goals—"big hairy audacious goals" as Jim Collins, author of *Good to Great*,[9] calls them—is pivotal to getting a team to want to work together, and then to getting them moving. A team with a stretch goal has a purpose that bonds them to-gether: It's easier to see how to best use everyone's talents, and the group can encourage each other through the challenges and share the wins. A team without a stretch goal is like a ship without a rudder. People wonder why they should bother working together, when they could be working on their own more efficiently. There needs to be a bigger challenge they can only achieve as a team.

As a leader sitting outside of the team you're in a great position to stretch the group. You can see what the team as a whole might be ca-pable of, better than those inside can. Setting stretch goals internally can be fraught with debate as people argue over what is realistic or too big a stretch. The CREATE model is a fantastic way to define stretch goals in a group: It's a way of structuring everyone's thinking. In this way the goals come from within the group, and you can be on the outside gently stretching them as the conversation unfolds.

Choose your focus

This is one of the most useful tools in this book for working with teams. Here are two examples of how you could use this model:

- At the start of every team meeting you could put up this model where people can see it, then work your way down from the top. Start a meeting with what the team vision or goal is, then recap on where you are in the planning process, all before getting into any details.
- Having this model visible in a meeting will help people recog-nize for themselves when they have got lost in problem or drama. When people see this for themselves they can quickly move back up to the planning or details, whichever is relevant.

Practice placement

Placement is a really useful skill for facilitating team conversations. Teams consist of many brains, with different expectations, fears, or filters. I find the more people I am working with, the more placement

I need to use so that the conversation stays on track. When I lead a team I find I do a lot of placement at the start, then stop regularly during the meeting, covering these types of issues:

- How long the meeting is running
- The goal for the meeting
- What the leader's role is
- What each person's role is
- The type of conversation we plan to have (e.g., brainstorming or goal setting)
- Any agreements we had made earlier about working together
- Anything from the last time we met so that everyone knows where the team is at now.

Without lots of placement when leading teams, the conversation can go all over the place. With six people in a team, an issue that was completely unnecessary to discuss could bounce around and chew up twenty minutes. Through the use of placement, meetings can be substantially more effective, completing in far less time than they normally take.

Clarify

Team discussions are complex, chaotic interactions. Someone might ask "What's the solution to our retention problem?" One person might get upset about the issue and talk about the way the company isn't taking care of anyone. This person can't be interrupted, or else they might get even more upset. Someone might complain about the money being spent on recruitment. Another is worried about morale. Another wants to sound smart so they'll get a promotion that's looming, and spouts lots of interesting but not very relevant industry data about the issue. Each person feels his or her point of view is the most important. People start to debate each other's perspectives and suddenly the whole thing is a mess. Using placement regularly to help everyone in the group stay on purpose helps, but so does clarifying powerfully as you go. Clarifying the group conversation as you go helps people see what the point of each discussion is, which helps the team self-correct and stay on course.

Clarifying completes a cycle of any dialogue, it brings a conclusion to a complex set of ideas by simplifying the conversation to the bottom line. Clarifying well as a team leader when people are having complex conversations can help you get a lot further in the conversations, spending less time on the details and more time on what's important. When you clarify, use as few words as possible and focus on the bottom line, the essence of what's being said. Statements about how the conversation is going can help—for example, "sounds like we're right off track here," or "sounds like this is a hot spot for several people," or "feels like it might be useful to get back to our plan for the meeting."

Follow the CREATE model

The CREATE model is so useful for improving the way a team thinks that I rarely start any kind of meeting without it. Imagine a team discussing a new organizational chart they are preparing. By following the CREATE model, the questions to start with include:

> "Where are we with the project so far?"
> "Can we define the current situation with this project, listing everything we know?"
> "Let's do a status report on exactly what has happened so far."
> "What's our goal again, and where are we up to in the plan?"
> "What do we want to achieve this meeting, specifically?"

By starting at the beginning, it's much easier to make informed choices about which path the group's thinking should take. I find when I launch into a meeting without these types of questions, the problems and dramas become the focus rather than the way forward.

Once you have a through understanding of the current reality, the next step is to explore different alternatives for how the team could think. Questions to ask here include:

"What's the best way for us to achieve our goal for this meeting?"

"Should we brainstorm or should we each share what we've prepared, any preferred options here?"

"How could we best think this through as a group from here?"

"Let's work out the best way we could move forward by throwing around a few options."

From here it becomes clear that there is an approach the group wants to follow, so we go in that direction, and tap the energy of the group. Here we might ask questions like:

"Who's the best person to focus on this action?"

"What do we need to do to ensure this happens?"

"Do we need to set a deadline?"

"What are the next steps here?"

The CREATE model is a way of structuring the thought processes of a group. Using this model instead of launching into a chaotic discussion gets everyone focused together, saves time, improves the quality of ideas, and energizes everyone.

All of the models in this book are going to be useful with teams; for now I just wanted to focus on the highlights. As my new neighbor discovered, most teams by nature are disjointed, chaotic systems with people pulling in many different directions. The job of the leader is to bring the team together. The best way to do this is by getting them to think in the most efficient and effective ways, by improving *all* their thinking—without telling anyone what to do.

USING THE SIX STEPS WITH CHILDREN

Focus is the quintessential component of superior performance in every activity, no matter what the level of skill or the age of the performer. Focus follows interest, and interest does not need coercion. A gentle hand on the steering wheel of attention will suffice.

TIM GALLWEY (2001)

Many otherwise intelligent adults fall in a heap when it comes to interacting with their teenage children. So "Can I use these principles with my kids?" is a question I often get asked.

The answer is: yes and no. Let's explore the "no" part first. When people ask this question, they are really asking, "Can you give me any tricks for controlling my teenager?" For these parents, the bad news is that the Six Steps won't help you control anyone. In fact, you could say the opposite is the case here: following the Six Steps requires that you let go of control, put aside your agenda, and trust that others will find the best answers to their questions inside themselves.

Now let me be very clear here. I am not advocating that we throw out the concept of discipline or boundaries. When your eighteen year old asks, "Can I borrow the car to get to a big party where I am planning to have a few drinks?" maybe the answer should come from you, not them. The teenage brain has not yet fully formed to know what's best for its own interests long term.[10]

Putting all that aside, the "yes" part of the question about the Six

Steps and kids is that these models can definitely make conversations with your teenager less charged, and even more fulfilling for both of you. Let's explore this a little.

Let them do all the thinking

There are, speaking very broadly, two types of brain. Firstly there are children's brains, from birth up to roughly age seven,[11] which take in everything around them and store information easily, seemingly effortlessly even. Watch a family with a five year old and an eight year old move to a foreign country and you will see the young one pick up the new language fluently and the elder one struggle for the rest of their life.

Then there are adult brains. Adult brains still take in new information, but at a slower rate. Adult learning theory[12] says that we learn as adults by making connections to existing information in our brains. We learn by looking at an idea and deciding on its relevance to us, its importance, its usefulness. If we like how this new piece of information fits our thinking, we decide to hardwire it into our circuits, through various conscious and unconscious activities. So the adult brain is proactive in the process and learns only when it chooses to. The child, however, will hear five languages and soak it all up. To put this another way, from about age seven, children only learn when they want to, no matter how many times you say something.

Changing the way your child behaves requires changing the way they think. Achieving this by saying, "Why don't you be more positive?" has about as much impact on a child as it does an adult. We need to get them doing more of the thinking, instead of just telling them what to do.

Give positive feedback

The importance of positive feedback for children is indisputable. There is even a direct and proven correlation between the amount of delight a mother exhibits when her offspring does something new and the future intelligence of her child.[13] Feedback generally isn't just helpful—it's essential to our well-being. Studies of children who had no feedback at all from others showed that both their development and their health were severely compromised. We need other people, interactions, to survive.

It's interesting to note that this is similar to the way the brain functions. A child is born with double the number of neurons it needs and its brain is then pruned according to use or disuse. In parts of the brain where no connections are made, where no flow of energy comes back from the outside world, that part of the brain simply withers away.

As a parent, we have so many opportunities for giving positive feedback. It's about noticing what children are doing well, even just what they are doing. Feedback can be as simple as:

"Thanks so much for remembering to take out the trash."

"I appreciate the way you cleaned your room without being asked."

"It was great the way you shared your toys with your friends."

"You were so courageous after that fall."

"You did really well."

"Great job."

"Well done."

There's a link here to the positive psychology[14] movement—a field committed to improving our well-being as individuals, groups, and as a society. A cornerstone of positive psychology is understanding one's strengths, and utilizing these strengths in all aspects of our lives. This is a different approach to trying to resolve our weaknesses. As parents, if we listen for potential with our children, we will hear their interests, their passions, the way their brains want to grow, and we can help them to foster these strengths in various ways, first by giving them lots of positive feedback.

Establish permission

Every time I introduce the concept of establishing permission to parents, several of them try this out and are delighted with the results. Without establishing permission, we can be launching into personal conversations whether our kids are ready to have a conversation or not. We don't ask if we can get personal, we just do it. So they push back.

It's not a big leap to ask permission. It could be as simple as this: "I'd like to have a chat with you about chores around the house; would it be okay to do that now or would it be better to make a time so we can talk about this properly?"

My favorite question here is "What if they say no?" because, of course, at times they will. Especially at first. Well, you always have the right to ask permission to ask permission again, a kind of "Is it okay if I ask you this again later?" question. I haven't heard of this failing yet.

Practice placement

In the chapter on giving feedback I introduced the idea that the more emotional charge there might be in a conversation, the more placement we should use. Tell me a conversation with more potential for emotional charge than trying to talk to a teenager about something they don't want to talk about! Once you have got permission to have a conversation, using placement can make a big difference to how that conversation might go. It gives you a chance to let the kids know where you are coming from before getting lost in the details, problems, or, of course, the drama. Here's an example of how this might work in a conversation:

I'd really like to talk about chores, but I know this is a difficult conversation that we've tried to have a few times and it hasn't gone well. We'd both prefer not to talk about this I'm sure . . . but I want to have this conversation in a different way today. I am not going to tell you what to do or how you should think, I simply want to work together on the solution to this issue, and explore a few different ideas. Would it be okay with you if we did that for a few minutes now?

Ask thinking questions

Asking questions is one of the few ways to facilitate learning in other people. Remember that asking thinking questions means you are not making people wrong, you are not telling them what to do in a tricky questioning format, and you are not looking to do any thinking yourself. Asking thinking questions means you are there to help people become more aware of their own thinking. Some examples of questions you might ask after permission and placement with a teenager might include:

> "How often do you think about this issue?"
> "How important is this issue to you?"
> "How could we best work this out—what do you think?"
> "How can I best help you think this through?"
> "What would be a great outcome of this conversation for you?"

Do these types of questions look familiar?

Create new thinking

A conversation to help a teenager think differently is going to work best by following the CREATE model. Let's look at an example conversation between a parent, Alicia, and her teenager, Mel. Alicia is worried that Mel's not applying herself at school and should be getting better grades. The issue has come up several times in conversations, resulting in slammed doors and sullen moods that lasted for days. Alicia has learned these new models and is tentatively trying a new approach.

Alicia: *Mel, I'd like to have a conversation about school, in a different way than we have up till now. Would you be willing to give this a go?*

Mel: *Why bother? We've fought about this for weeks already.*

Alicia: *I know we've had a rough time trying to talk about this, but I want to have a different type of conversation. I am not going to tell you what to do. Instead, I want to understand your thinking more.*

Mel: *Umm . . . okay, that sounds different . . .*

Alicia: *First, I want you to know that I want this conversation to be productive for both of us, and if it feels like it stops being that way for either of us let's stop and take stock. I also want to apologize for being on your case and giving you a hard time about school. It's obviously been tough somehow. I do want the best for you, and perhaps I want it so much I have not been listening very well.*

Mel: *Well, okay, you've got my attention. . . . I had a whole list of items I wanted to tell you but they seem to have gone out the window now.*

When we realize we've been using an approach with our kids that's doomed to fail, like trying to tell them what to do, perhaps the best thing to do is just apologize. Apologizing can pull the rug out from underneath emotional tension, bringing intimacy back into a difficult relationship.

Alicia: *How are you feeling about how your school is going? I promise it's not a loaded question, I really just want to listen.*

Mel: *Well, it's going okay, it's just that . . .*

Alicia: *I want you to be comfortable sharing everything with me, I promise not to get mad whatever you say.*

Mel: *Okay, well, the thing is, since I started getting better grades and got lifted to a higher class, everything has changed. Now I don't get on with two teachers, and I have hardly any of my old friends in these classes. I want to do well but I am missing my friends, and missing having people to do homework with like we used to do last year.*

Alicia: *Wow, I had no idea this was going on.*

Mel: *Yeah, well, it's been tough and I haven't had anyone to talk to about this.*

They talk for a while about what's been happening, then Alicia asks if Mel is okay to explore some ideas together. Some of the questions Alicia might ask in the current reality phase of the conversation include:

"How long have you been upset by this?"

"How important is this to you?"

"What impact is it having on your schoolwork, on a scale of one to ten?"

"How do you feel about what you've tried so far to resolve this?"

"How can I best help you with this?"

It turns out that Mel has been upset by this all year, it has been distracting her every day, it was the most stressful thing at school, and it has been impacting her work at an eight on a scale of one to ten. Mel feels guilty about how little she's done to resolve the issue, which was only to ask one teacher what options she might have to swap classes. Mel realized that she needed to do something about the situation, got committed, and was ready to think through some options.

In the explore alternatives phase, Alicia could ask questions like:

"What would it take to sort this out, do you have all the information you need or do you need to do some research?"

"What process might you need to follow to decide on how to move forward?"

"How can I best help you think through what to do next?"

In this case Mel realized there were many creative options she hadn't explored. She acknowledged she hadn't started to think about solutions because she was blaming the school. She quickly realized there might be other ways to connect with her old friends, by starting a special interest group, or joining the school play together.

In the tap their energy phase, Alicia helped Mel commit to following up her insight, which was to talk to her friends and find options for staying connected. She also realized there might be people in her new classes that she could be friends with, and decided to pay more attention to who was in her class and reach out to connect to new people.

No one could have guessed what Mel's problem was, nor tell her what she should be doing about this. By taking Mel through a process of discovering her own answers, Alicia did a great job of helping Mel be the best she could be, while deepening the trust and respect in their relationship.

Many parents tell me their home environment has shifted dramatically through having these types of conversations. (Notice I didn't say "to a world of love and harmony"—these are teenagers, after all!) Maybe it's time parents went back to school to learn how to bring out the best in their kids. It doesn't take much to develop new habits: intention, commitment, and a little focus, and we have new wiring before we know it.

APPLYING THE SIX STEPS
TO A WHOLE ORGANIZATION

If you don't like the way the world is, you change it.
You have an obligation to change it. Just do it one step at a time.

MARIAN WRIGHT EDELMAN (2000)

There's another whole book I'd like to write about applying the principles of Quiet Leadership to a whole organization, looking at how to transform leaders at every level. At this stage of this book I'd just like to introduce some high-level ideas.

First, I believe that organizations can change. However, just like an individual, and like the brain itself, an organization can only be changed from the inside out. It won't change because people tell it to—it needs to have wide-scale insights by itself, and through this process, make deep new connections. For an organization to change, it needs to create new maps to define how information flows between people and systems. And it needs these maps to become the dominant pathways along which resources flow. This requires—just as in the brain—attention, time, and lots of positive feedback. This attention and positive feedback can't come from just a few select individuals at senior levels. For an organization to embrace any kind of deep change, thousands of its people need to become champions of a new way.

The old way, that of telling people what to do, was embedded in our culture at a time when it was thought that our humanity was best left at home. This old way is beginning to look tired and ineffective. The new way, the way of a Quiet Leader, is to artfully build on people's strengths by improving their thinking. Doing this requires a basic understanding of the way our brain works, a deep respect for the brain's ability to solve any problem, and a certain graciousness and humility that is obvious in some of our more successful leaders.

Of course, changing to any kind of new way is no easy task. What's required is a real passion, a long-term vision, an excellent plan, sufficient resources, and a whole lot of courage. There are battles to be fought and problems and dramas to wade through. However, as with an individual brain, if you look at an organization and strain to listen for its potential, you may just start to see positive change unfolding before your very eyes. And as you see it, so shall it become.

IN CONCLUSION

*A knowledge of brain science will provide one of
the major foundations of the new age to come.*

GERALD EDELMAN (1995)

I opened this book with a story about an organization that needed to redefine the way its people spoke to one another. The woman showing me around was unsure if this was even remotely possible.

Yet as we've learned, change is more than possible: It's happening inside us at an extraordinary pace, with millions of new connections created every second inside our head. Our brain is constantly looking to improve its own structure in any way that will make the world it interacts with more cohesive.

As leaders managing people who are paid to think, it's time we learned more about how to improve the thing we're paying for—not people's shoulders or hands, but their minds and brains. It's time we better harness the power of the most complex and adaptive bit of technology in the known universe.

In doing so we will begin to resolve many of the big challenges faced by organizations today: the lack of engagement in the workplace, the challenges of developing new generations of leaders, and the need for continuous innovation just to stay in business.

Perhaps by learning to lead with the brain in mind we will do much more as well. Perhaps, to paraphrase Theodore Zeldin, our humanity will start to catch up with our technology.

GLOSSARY OF TERMS

I have summarized the key concepts discussed in this book for easy reference, in three categories: the central models and ideas I developed, such as "placement"; two-part distinctions I used throughout the book, for example, "interesting versus useful"; and the main scientific terms. You will also find other resources at www.quietleadership.com.

CENTRAL MODELS AND IDEAS

I have categorized these by chapter for easy reference.

About the Six Steps

Path of least resistance: A term coined by Robert Fritz, which I have applied to having conversations with others. It means the shortest distance (in time and effort) to get from point A (wanting to have a positive impact on someone) to point B (having a positive impact on someone).

STEP 1: Think About Thinking

Let them do all the thinking: One of the central principles in this book. The best way to improve performance is by helping people think better; doing this requires letting other people think, then helping them think in more efficient ways, instead of telling people what to do.

Focus on solutions: Being solution-focused means focusing only on the way ahead. Looking into the problem reinforces the brain circuits associated with the problem. Focusing on solutions is a step toward creating new mental maps.

Remember to stretch: Any time we try a new activity, behavior, or way of thinking, we are literally forging a new pathway in our brain, creating circuits that don't currently exist. Doing this takes energy and focus, and requires intensive use of our conscious mind. Leaders can help bring about change and make change long lasting by stretching people, and normalizing the emotions they may feel along the way.

Accentuate the positive: We're all our own worst critics. What we need more of is positive feedback, especially when we are learning a new behavior or habit. Positive feedback helps embed new mental maps.

Put process before content: Having a clear structure for a conversation helps move the conversation forward smoothly. We start by asking permission and agreeing to a context for the conversation. Then we follow the Dance of Insight model (placement ➜ ask thinking questions ➜ clarifying).

Choose your focus: This model helps us with all of step one. It helps us think about thinking, and focus on solutions, and stretch, and have good process. The Choose Your Focus model describes five mental frames we can approach any situation from: vision; planning; detail; problem; and drama. Having a simple, easy-to-remember model helps us see our mode of thinking quickly, and then choose a more useful way of thinking. This model has wide application in the workplace.

STEP 2: Listen for Potential

Listening for potential: This means listening generously with the certainty that the person speaking can and will solve their own dilemmas, because the answers are within them. It means listening for people's own insights, energy, possibilities, passion, and future.

The clarity of distance: Leaders can be more helpful if they stay out of the details and interact with their people at a high level, looking for patterns and qualities in activities that can't be seen when we are too close. We get too close when we have too much detail, see things through our own filters, have an agenda, or get engaged by strong emotions.

STEP 3: Speak with Intent

Succinct: Quiet Leaders are succinct when they speak. They are able to communicate their ideas using very few words.

Specific: Quiet Leaders are specific when they speak. They are able to figure out and communicate the core of the idea they want to transmit.

Generous: Quiet Leaders are generous when the speak. They speak so that the listener can immediately understand and relate to the concepts they want to communicate.

STEP 4: Dance Toward Insight

The four faces of insight: This describes what goes on when you look at people's faces, before, while, and after they have an insight. There are specific mental functions occurring in the brain during insights that give off energy, which you can see if you look for them. The four steps are: awareness of a dilemma; reflection; illumination; and motivation.

Awareness of a dilemma: A dilemma is defined as being between two opposing desires and not knowing which way to turn. This book posits that dilemmas are mental maps in conflict, and the leader's job is to help people create new ways of reconnecting their thinking through the moment of illumination.

Reflection: This occurs when we ask questions that make people think deeply. People need time to reflect to be able to make new connections. The brain gives off alpha-band waves when we reflect.

Illumination: This is the moment when a new map is created. Gamma-band waves are seen in the brain at this moment.

Motivation: This is the moment immediately following an illumination. We are energized by a new insight, and have neurotransmitters coursing through our brain, inspiring us to want to do something. However, the effects of these chemicals pass quickly.

The Dance of Insight: This is the structure of the conversation we follow in order to elicit insights from others. It's composed of: permission; placement; thinking questions; and clarifying.

Permission: We ask permission before going into a deeper, more personal layer of a conversation. Every time there may be an emotional response to what we are going to say, we ask permission first. Permission lets people feel safer, builds trust, and allows you to ask hard questions.

Placement: When we are having a conversation, it's very useful to make sure that both parties are coming from the "same place." Placement is like a combination of setting the scene plus full disclosure plus a statement of intent. Placement gets the other person to start thinking.

Repeated placement: We keep placing people in conversations every question or so, to remind both parties about where they are and where they're trying to get to. This helps both people stay more on track.

Thinking questions: These are questions designed to elicit insight: They bring about re-flection, which creates more self-awareness, generating a greater sense of responsibility. Thinking questions are not "why" questions; they are "how" questions.

Clarifying: This is being able to extract the essence of what someone says, focused at a very high level, and feed it back to them in a couple of words. Clarifying is about identifying learning and emotions. We give people mini insights when we clarify well.

STEP 5: CREATE New Thinking

CREATE model: This describes the different phases in a conversation to improve people's thinking, following the path of least resistance. It stands for **C**urrent **R**eality, **E**xplore **A**lternatives, and **T**ap Their **E**nergy.

Desired outcome: This is the collection of ideas, thoughts, facts, and emotions that you'd expect to have if you accomplished something that's important to you.

Current reality: The first element in the CREATE model. Here we focus on identifying the landscape of people's thinking, to identify qualities of their thinking to help them reflect and bring about an illumination.

Explore alternatives: The second element in the CREATE model. This is when we open up lots of possibilities in a conversation, exploring many ways forward.

Tap their energy: The third element in the CREATE model. The energy that is released after having an insight needs to be put into action immediately, so we tap this energy while it's there, getting people to flesh out their ideas while they are fresh and commit to taking specific actions.

STEP 6: Follow Up

FEELING model: This is a way of following up on actions people set for themselves, to bring about the creation of new circuits. It stands for Facts, Emotions, Encourage, Learning, Implications, and New Goal.

Using the Six Steps to Give Feedback

Giving feedback for great performance: Give extensive positive feedback, being very specific about what they did well and what impact this has. This is also an excellent opportunity to use the Six Steps to dig down further and identify new habits people are developing, to help them grow and develop further.

Giving feedback for below-par performance: Defuse any emotional tension, then use the Six Steps to help people identify for themselves what they have learned, and what new habits they can create moving forward.

Giving feedback for poor performance: Emotional tension needs to be carefully defused, then again use the Six Steps to help people identify their learning and the new habits they need moving forward.

TWO-PART DISTINCTIONS USED THROUGHOUT THE BOOK

Process versus Content: When a leader is having a conversation to help someone think something through, it's important that the leader focus on the process rather than the content of the conversation.

Explicit versus Implicit: In order for something to be made explicit, it needs to be said aloud, with words (for example, during placement). Making things explicit frees up everyone's neurons to focus on central issues, because we are less distracted by uncertainties.

Interesting versus Useful: Discussing problems is interesting. Discussing solutions is useful. When something is interesting, we don't put much energy into memorizing it. But when something is useful, we consciously make the effort to learn it so that we can apply the learning elsewhere.

Deconstruct versus Reconstruct: Deconstructing hard wiring in the brain is very difficult (when we try to eliminate ingrained habits). It's much easier to create (reconstruct) new wiring, and create new habits.

Why versus Learning: There are two types of questions you can ask of others. Those with the word "why" in them usually don't lead to learning; they lead to reasons and justifications. Learning questions help people make new connections, by bringing about new insight.

Intent versus Impact: Sometimes the intent that we have in a conversation is not achieved and the conversation has an undesired impact on the other person.

Thinking versus Thinking About Thinking: Thinking about an issue a person has means we come up with ideas for others. Thinking about thinking means thinking to figure out what questions to ask that will help the person come up with their own insights. The leader is focused on the person, not the issue on the table.

KEY SCIENTIFIC TERMS

Neuron: The neuron is the primary cell for the human nervous system. There are more than 100 billion neurons in the brain itself, with more than 100 trillion connections (synapses) linking them.

Synapse: The synapse is the juncture, or main connection point, between our neurons. Neurons form connections (circuits) based on the electrical and chemical signals across synapses.

Maps: Gerald Edelman coined the term. A map is a description of how our neurons are connected. We have maps of neurons, then maps of these maps, and maps of these maps, and so on. The word "map" can be replaced by neural circuitry, neural pathway, circuit, wiring, or connection.

Working memory: This refers to our ability to hold information in our conscious mind. Our working memory is relatively tiny, holding small groups of about seven ideas at one time. Grouping ideas helps us remember more. Working memory tends to disappear after a short time; we don't remember a phone number we dial once, for example, although we remember the number while dialing it.

Hard wiring: Hard wiring refers to thoughts, skills, or memories that remain with us for some time. The scientific term for this is long-term potentiation (LTP). LTP is a form of neuroplasticity. It occurs when two or more neurons are active at the same time, which strengthens their connections. Long-term can mean anything from minutes to hours, days, weeks—right up to a lifetime.

Neuroplasticity: The ability of the brain to rewire itself based on where we focus attention. Genes dictate the overall architecture of the brain, but within that structure the system is highly flexible.

Neural Darwinism: Gerald Edelman came up with this concept in his 1987 book, *Neural Darwinism: The Theory of Neuronal Group Selection.* It refers to the fact that synapses that are used the most are kept, while those used least are destroyed or pruned. This on-going process determines our neural pathways.

Attention: Where we choose to focus our attention increases the connections in this part of the brain.

fMRI: Functional Magnetic Resonance Imaging. A machine that measures changes in the blood flow through any part of our body, using strong magnets. Significant breakthrough research has been done on the brain since the introduction of fMRI technologies.

Ambient neural activity: This refers to the way our neurons are always carrying some electrical activity due to internal events. These internal signals sometimes become too strong and don't allow external signals to be processed. Neurons have a cap on the level of impulses they can process, and can be easily overloaded.

Alpha-band waves: A specific frequency given off by the brain. Some of the best leaders exhibit a lot of alpha waves. Alpha waves occur when we are relaxed and centered, and just before we have an insight.

Gamma-band waves: These occur during the moment of illumination. Gamma-band waves can signify parts of the brain connecting up.

Reframing: When we look at a situation from another perspective, we are reframing.

Phases of change: A model that illustrates how we feel when we try a new activity, the different emotions we experience. Knowing these phases helps to normalize the experience. The model consists of unconscious incompetence, conscious incompetence, conscious competence, and unconscious competence.

Cognitive-Behavioral Therapy: A structured psychotherapeutic method used to modify undesired attitudes and behaviors by identifying and replacing negative thoughts and changing the rewards for behaviors.

Solutions-Focused Therapy: A therapeutic method that assumes the client is the expert and has strengths and capacities that can be accessed to make her or his life more satisfactory. The therapist magnifies client strengths, resources, and past successes, which leads to the construction of solutions.

Behavioral Science: A scientific discipline such as sociology, anthropology, or psychology, in which the actions and reactions of humans and animals are studied through observational and experimental methods.

Positive Psychology: The study of the mind based on researching happiness and well-being instead of sickness. An emerging new field in psychology.

Flow: Coined by Mihaly Csikszentmihalyi for the zone of peak performance that occurs between boredom and too much stress.

RESOURCES

BOOKS

If you would like to do any related reading, I have selected below a few of the most relevant and important books, in addition to a full list of references coming up. The books are roughly in the order of how relevant they are to this book itself.

The brain

John J. Ratey, *A User's Guide to the Brain: Perception, Attention, and the Four Theaters of the Brain* (New York: Vintage Books, 2002)

Jeffrey M. Schwartz and Sharon Begley, *The Mind & The Brain: Neuroplasticity and the Power of Mental Force* (New York: HarperCollins Publishers, Regan Books, 2002)

Leslie Brothers, M.D., *Friday's Footprint: How Society Shapes the Human Mind* (New York: Oxford University Press, 1997)

Gerald M. Edelman, *Bright Air, Brilliant Fire: On the Matter of the Mind* (New York: Basic Books, 1992)

Jeff Hawkins with Sandra Blakeslee, *On Intelligence* (New York: Times Books, Henry Holt and Company, 2004)

Joseph Ledoux, *Synaptic Self: How Our Brains Become Who We Are* (New York: Viking Penguin, 2002)

Thomas B. Czerner, *What Makes You Tick: The Brain in Plain English* (Hoboken: Wiley, 2002)

Leadership development

Ram Charan, Stephen Drotter, and James Noel, *The Leadership Pipeline: How to Build the Leadership-Powered Company* (San Francisco: Jossey-Bass, 2001)

Louis Carter, David Ulrich, and Marshall Goldsmith, *Best Practices in Leadership Development and Organization Change: How the Best Companies Ensure Meaningful Change and Sustainable Leadership* (Hoboken: Wiley, 2005)

Bill George, Authentic Leadership: Rediscovering the Secrets to Creating Lasting Value (San Francisco: Jossey-Bass, 2003)

Stephen R. Covey, The 8th Habit: From Effectiveness to Greatness (New York: Free Press, 2004)

Coaching

David Rock, Personal Best: Step by Step Coaching for Creating the Life You Want (Australia: Simon & Schuster, 2001)

Dianna Anderson and Merril Anderson, Coaching that Counts: Harness the Power of Leadership Coaching to Deliver Strategic Value (Hoboken: Wiley, 2005)

W. Timothy Gallwey, The Inner Game of Tennis (New York: Random House, 1974)

The science of coaching

David Rock, Foundations to Coaching (Hoboken: John Wiley & Sons, forthcoming)

Bruce Peltier, The Psychology of Executive Coaching (Ann Arbor: Sheridan Books, 2001).

Positive psychology

Mihaly Csikszentmihalyi, Flow: The Psychology of Optimal Experience (New York: HarperCollins Publishers, 1990)

Martin Seligman, Learned Optimism (New York: Free Press, 1998)

Philosophy

Theodore Zeldin, An Intimate History of Humanity (New York: HarperCollins Publishers, Harper Perennial, 1996)

Theodore Zeldin, Conversation: How Talk Can Change Our Lives (New York: Hidden Spring, 2000)

JOURNALS AND WEB SITES

www.quietleadership.com

International Journal of Evidence-Based Coaching and Mentoring, www.brookes.ac.uk/schools/education/ijebcm

International Journal of Coaching in Organizations, www.ijco.info

RESULTS COACHING SYSTEMS

Corporate programs: www.workplacecoaching.com

Public programs: www.resultscoaches.com

NOTES

WHY SHOULD LEADERS CARE ABOUT IMPROVING THINKING?

1. *The Daily Mail,* London (October 17, 2001).
2. Interpolated from statement: "Of all US workers 18 or older, 55% are not engaged, 19% actively disengaged, 26% engaged." Gallup Poll (March 15, 2001).
3. P. J. Miscovich, *The New Knowledge Workplace* (2005). Accessed at www .pwcglobal.com/extweb/newcolth.nsf/docid/B847266B96111E6785256 FD400623C5C?OpenDocument.
4. The iceberg is a metaphor that helps to understand the topography of human behavior. Six sevenths of an iceberg are under water and remain unseen—while determining the size and the manner in which the iceberg acts at the same time. This model has also been used to illustrate Freud's model of the human mind: www.wilderdom.com/personality/ L8-3TopographyMindIceberg.html, and to understand conflict dynamics: www.dadalos.org/frieden_int/grundkurs_4/eisberg.htm, for example.
5. Ram Charan, Stephen Drotter, and James Noel, *The Leadership Pipeline: How to Build the Leadership-Powered Company* (San Francisco: Jossey-Bass, 2001).

PART ONE: RECENT DISCOVERIES ABOUT THE BRAIN THAT CHANGE EVERYTHING

1. John J. Ratey, *A User's Guide to the Brain* (New York: Vintage Books, 2001); Gerald M. Edelman, *Neural Darwinism: The Theory of Neuronal Group Selection* (New York: Basic Books, 1987); and Jeff Hawkins with Sandra Blakeslee, *On Intelligence* (New York: Times Books, 2004).
2. The first use of the word "maps" for how we think was by Nobel laureate Gerald Edelman, part of a whole theory called neural Darwinism. See also

his book *Bright Air, Brilliant Fire: On the Matter of the Mind* (New York: Basic Books, 1992).

3. Ansel L. Woldt and Sarah M. Toman, eds., *Gestalt Therapy: History, Theory, and Practice* (Thousand Oaks, CA: SAGE Publications, 2005); Joseph Zinker, *Creative Process in Gestalt Therapy* (New York: Vintage Books, 1978).

4. Hawkins and Blakeslee, *On Intelligence.*

5. See www.crystalinks.com/archimedes.html.

6. For an excellent and comprehensive text on the human brain, see Rita Carter, *Mapping the Mind* (Berkeley: University of California Press, 1999).

7. Ratey, *A User's Guide.*

8. D. Dobbs, "Fact or Phrenology?" *Scientific American Mind,* 16, no. 1 April 2005: 24–31.

9. James L. McGaugh, *Memory and Emotion: The Making of Lasting Memories* (New York: Columbia University Press, 2003).

10. Joseph LeDoux, *Synaptic Self: How Our Brains Become Who We Are* (New York: Viking Penguin, 2002).

11. John G. Milton, Steven S. Small and Ana Solodkin, "On the Road to Automatic Dynamic Aspects in the Development of Expertise," *Journal of Clinical Neurophysiology,* 21 (May/June 2004): 133–227.

12. Commonly attributed to Anaïs Nin.

13. V. S. Ramachandran and Sandra Blakeslee, *Phantoms in the Brain: Probing the Mysteries of the Human Mind* (New York: HarperCollins Publishers, 1999); V. S. Ramachandran, *A Brief Tour of Human Consciousness: From Impostor Poodles to Purple Numbers* (New York: Pi Press, 2005).

14. "As strange as it sounds, when your own behavior is involved, your predictions not only precede sensation, they determine sensation. Thinking of going to the next pattern in a sequence causes a cascading prediction of what you should experience next. As the cascading prediction unfolds, it generates the motor commands necessary to fulfill the prediction. Thinking, predicting, and doing are all part of the same unfolding of sequences moving down the cortical hierarchy. 'Doing' by thinking, the parallel unfolding of perception and motor behavior, is the essence of what is called goal-oriented behavior." Hawkins and Blakeslee, *On Intelligence,* 158.

15. Most wars are fought in the name of a mental model. Religion, politics, and even patriotism are, at least from a neuroscience perspective, all mental models that influence the way we see the world.

16. Jeffrey M. Schwartz with Beverly Beyette, *Brain Lock: Free Yourself from Obsessive-Compulsive Behavior* (New York: HarperCollins Publishers, Regan Books, 1996).

17. James Claiborn and Cherry Pedrick, *The Habit Change Workbook: How to Break Bad Habits and Form Good Ones* (Oakland, CA: New Harbinger Publications, 2001).

18. T. P. Pons, P. E. Garraghty, A. K. Ommaya, J. H. Haas, E. Taub, and M. Mishkin, "Massive cortical reorganization after sensory deafferentation in adult macaques," *Science*, 252 (June 28, 1991): 1857–1860; M. M. Merzenich, G. Recanzone, W. M. Jenkins, T. T. Allard, and R. J. Nudo, "Cortical Plasticity," in P. Rakic and W. Singer, eds., *Neurobiology of Neocortex* (Hoboken: John Wiley & Sons: 1988): 41–67; M. M. Merzenich, G. Recanzone, W. M. Jenkins, and R. J. Nudo, "How the Brain Functionally Rewires Itself," in M. Arbib and J. Robinson, eds., *Natural and Artificial Parallel Computations* (Cambridge, MA: MIT Press, 1990): 177–210.

19. Merzenich et al., "Cortical Plasticity."

20. See note 18 above. See also Joachim Liepert, Heike Bauder, Wolfgang H. R. Miltner, Edward Taub, Cornelius Weiller, "Treatment-Induced Cortical Reorganization After Stroke in Humans," *Stroke* 31, no. 6 (2000): 1210–1216.

21. When the brain learns, the connections between neurons (synapses) get stronger. See N. Toni, P. A. Buchs, I. Nikonenko, C. R. Bron, and D. Muller, "LTP promotes formation of multiple spine synapses between a single axon terminal and a dendrite," *Nature* 402 (November 25, 1999: 421–425; Maletic-Savatic, M., Malinow, R. and Svoboda, K. (1999) "Rapid Deudritic Morphogenesis in CA1 Hippocampal Dendrites Luduced by Synaptic Activity" *Science* 283, 1923–1927; Rafael Yuste and Tobias Bonhoeffer, "Morphological Changes in Dendritic Spines Associated with Long-Term Synaptic Plasticity," *Annual Review of Neuroscience* 24 (March 2001): 1071–1089. Scientific research is now showing that our synapses both chemically and structurally reshape when they strengthen in as quickly as one hour. See S. H. Shi, Y. Hayashi, R. S. Petralia, S. H. Zaman, R. J. Wenthold, K. Svoboda, and R. Malinow, "Rapid Spine Delivery and Redistribution of AMPA Receptors after Synaptic MNDA Receptor Activation," *Science* 284 (June 11, 1999): 1811–1816. One very important implication from these data is that we can create new habits remarkably quickly.

22. See Part One note 1. See also Jeffrey M. Schwartz and Sharon Begley, *The Mind and the Brain: Neuroplasticity and the Power of Mental Force* (New York: HarperCollins Publishers, Regan Books, 2002).

23. Jeffrey M. Schwartz with Beverly Beyette, *Brain Lock: Free Yourself from Obsessive-Compulsive Behavior.*

24. See Part One notes 1 and 2.

PART TWO: THE SIX STEPS TO TRANSFORMING PERFORMANCE

1. Schwartz and Begley, *The Mind and the Brain.*
2. Ratey, *A User's Guide;* Edelman, *Neural Darwinism;* Hawkins and Blakeslee, *On Intelligence;* Schwartz and Begley, *The Mind and the Brain.*
3. Martin E. P. Seligman, "Building human strength: psychology's forgotten mission," *Monitor on Psychology* 29, no. 1 (January 1998) and "Positive social science" *Monitor on Psychology* 29, no. 4 (April 1998), accessed at www.dokimos.ca/Co351.htm.
4. Paul Z. Jackson and Mark McKergow, *The Solutions Focus: The Simple Way to Positive Change* (London: Nicholas Brealey Publishing, 2002).
5. Schwartz and Begley, *The Mind and the Brain.*
6. Alan Deutschman, "Change or Die," *Fast Company* 94 (May 2005): 53 accessed at www.fastcompany.com/magazine/94/open_change-or-die.html.
7. W. Timothy Gallwey, *The Inner Game of Tennis* (New York: Random House, 1974).
8. William Bridges, *Managing Transitions: Making the Most of Change,* 2nd edition (Cambridge, MA: DaCapo Press, 2003); J. O. Prochaska and W. F. Velicer, "The Transtheoretical Model of Health Behavior Change," *American Journal of Health Promotion* 12, no. 1 (September-October 1997): 38–48.
9. F. Dimeo, M. Bauer, I. Varahram, G. Proest, U. Halter, "Benefits from Aerobic Exercise in Patients with Major Depression: a Pilot Study," *British Journal of Sports Medicine* 35 (April 2001): 114–117.
10. Mihaly Csikszentmihalyi, *Flow: The Psychology of Optimal Experience* (New York: HarperCollins Publishers, 1990).
11. Benson Smith, "Are You a Winning Coach?" *Gallup Management Journal* (October 14, 2004).
12. Gallwey, *Inner Game of Tennis.*
13. Ratey, *A User's Guide.*
14. L. Hubbs-Tait, A. M. Culp, R. E. Culp, and C. E. Miller, "Relation of Maternal Cognitive Stimulation, Emotional Support, and Intrusive Behavior during Head Start to Children's Kindergarten Cognitive Abilities," *Child Development* 73 no. 1 (January-February 2002): 110–131; T. Berry Brazelton, *Touchpoints: Your Child's Emotional and Behavioral Development* (Reading, MA: Perseus Books, 1992).
15. Carol S. Dweck, *Self-Theories: Their Role in Motivation, Personality, and Development* (London: Psychology Press, 1999).
16. Marshall Goldsmith, "Try Feedforward instead of Feedback," accessed at www.marshallgoldsmith.com/articles/article.asp?a_id=3.

17. Kenneth Blanchard and Spencer Johnson, *The One Minute Manager* (New York: William Morrow, 1981).
18. Ratey, *A User's Guide.*
19. Hawkins and Blakeslee, *On Intelligence.*
20. Schwartz and Begley, *The Mind and the Brain.*
21. Malcolm Gladwell, *Blink* (New York: Little, Brown, 2005).
22. Daniel Goleman, *Emotional Intelligence* (New York: Bantam, 1995).
23. It's widely accepted that we think at about 600 words per minute. That's four times faster than most speakers can talk.
24. Molly Bang, *Picture This: How Pictures Work* (New York: North-South Books, SeaStar Books, 2000).
25. The New York University/Results Coaching Systems Coaching Research Team: Marisa Galisteo, PhD; Jen Bieber; Christine Cookman; Erika Levasseur; Rose Rubin; Frank Mosca, PhD; Christine Ulrich, PhD; Miki Adcock; and Renee Sussman.
26. Mark Jung-Beeman, Edward M. Bowden, Jason Haberman, Jennifer L. Frymiare, Stella Arambel-Liu, Richard Greenblatt, Paul J. Reber, and John Kounios, "Neural Activity When People Solve Verbal Problems with Insight," *Public Library of Science Biology* 2 no. 4 (April 2004): e97, accessed at http://biology.plosjournals.org/perlserv/?request=get=docu ment&doi=10.1371/journal.pbio.0020097
27. Robert J. Sternberg and Janet E. Davidson, eds., *The Nature of Insight* (Cambridge, MA: MIT Press, 1996); Jing Luo, Kazuhis Niki, and Steven Phillips, "Neural Correlates of the "Aha! Reaction," *NeuroReport* 15 no. 13 (September 15, 2004): 2013–2017.
28. The Four Faces of Insight is similar to models developed by others. Graham Wallas, in his 1926 book *The Art of Thought* proposed the now commonly used creative model with the elements of Preparation, Incubation, Illumination, and Verification. There are other models that have explored the phases of change, such as the one by William Bridges and the Transtheoretical or "Stages to Change" model by James Prochaska.
29. Jung-Beeman et al, "Neural Activity."
30. www.biocybernaut.com
31. www.biocybernaut.com
32. www.biocybernaut.com
33. See note 27 above.
34. G. Csibra, G. Davis, M. W. Spratling and M. H. Johnson "Gamma Oscillations and Object Processing in the Infant Brain," *Science* vol. 290 (November 2000): 1582–1585.
35. See www.crystalinks.com/archimedes.html.

36. Dr. Margaret Paterson in collaboration with biochemist Dr. Ifor Capel at the Marie Curie Cancer Care in Surrey, England, showed in the early eighties (1983) that certain frequencies in the brain dramatically speed up production of a variety of neurotransmitters, different frequencies triggering different brain chemicals. For instance, a 10 Hz (alpha) signal boosts the production and turnover rate of serotonin, a chemical messenger that increases relaxation and eases pain, while catceholamines, vital for memory and learning, respond at around 4 Hz (theta).

37. Jung-Beeman et al, "Neural Activity."

38. See note 34.

39. Ratey, *A User's Guide.*

40. www.cba.uni.edu/buscomm/nonverbal/culture.html

41. 'Focusing attention was the critical action effecting neuroplastic changes in the cortex.' Pg 339, *The Mind and the Brain* (2002) Harper Collins, New York.

42. Weiss, A. *Beginning Mindfulness: Learning the Way of Awareness,* (Novato, California: Publishers Group West, 2004). Ellen J. Langer, *Mindfulness* (Perseus Books, 1989).

43. See note 41 above.

44. Olivero, G., Bane, K. D., Kopelman, R. E. (1997) "Executive Coaching as a transfer of training tool: Effects on productivity in a public agency" Public Personnel Management 26, 461–469. The study looked at training alone versus training plus coaching, and found that adding follow up coaching increased productivity by 88 percent, versus 28 percent of training alone.

45. Schwartz and Begley, *The Mind and the Brain.*

46. This is counter to standard management practice, which, based on a behaviorist view, says we should punish poor performance in some way.

PART THREE: PUTTING THE SIX STEPS TO USE

1. Ratey, *A User's Guide.*

2. Darren M. Lipnicki and Don G. Byrne, "Thinking on Your Back: Solving Anagrams Faster When Supine Than When Standing," *Cognitive Brain Research,* 24 no. 3 (August 2005): 719–722.

3. Mount Eliza Business School, Melbourne, Australia, 2003 leadership report.

4. Imperato, G., "How to Give Good Feedback," *Fast Company,* no. 17 (September 1998): 144.

5. Smith, B., *Are You a Winning Coach?, Gallup Management Journal,* no. 14 (October 2004).

6. Rath, T., *The Best Ways to Recognize Employees, Gallup Management Journal*, no. 9 (December 2004).
7. The largest study ever conducted on workplace satisfaction (Gallup, 1999) found that the development of social relationships was one of the most important factors in employee satisfaction and retention. The same study also found that praise and recognition were ranked among the top five building blocks of a profitable, productive work environment.
8. Daniel Goleman, *Emotional Intelligence* (New York: Bantam, 1995).
9. Jim Collins, *Good to Great: Why Some Companies Make the Leap . . . and Others Don't* (New York: HarperCollins, 2001).
10. Beckman, M., "Neuroscience, Crime, Culpability, and the Adolescent Brain," *Science* vol. 305, (2004): 596–599.
11. Ratey, *A User's Guide.*
12. Committee on Developments in the Science of Learning; John D. Bransford, Ann L. Brown, and Rodney R. Cocking, eds., with additional material from the Committee on Learning Research and Educational Practice; M. Suzanne Donovan, John D. Bransford, and James W. Pellegrino, eds,; National Research Council, *How People Learn: Brain, Mind, Experience, and School* (Washington, DC: National Academies Press, 2000).
13. See Part Two, note 14 above.
14. Csikszentmihalyi, M., *Flow: The Psychology of Optimal Experience* (New York: HarperCollins, 1990); Martin E. P. Seligman, *Learned Optimism: How to Change Your Mind and Your Life* (New York: Free Press, 1998); Seligman, *Authentic Happiness: Using the New Positive Psychology to Realize Your Potential for Lasting Fulfillment* (New York: Free Press, 2004).

INDEX

Page numbers in *italics* refer to illustrations.

ABOUT THE AUTHOR

David Rock is a global thought leader in the performance coaching field. During the 1990s he developed a coaching model that has since been taught to more than five thousand professionals in more than fifteen countries.

David is the founder of Results Coaching Systems (RCS), a global consulting and training organization operating in the United States, Europe, South Africa, Asia, Australia, and New Zealand. RCS has Fortune 100 clients in banking, insurance, and technology, and works extensively with large government agencies. David's work with organizations involves bringing about culture change through the strategic integration of a brain-based approach to leadership development and coaching.

RCS also provides internationally accredited coach training programs to the public in six global markets, training hundreds of executive and business coaches each year.

As an adjunct lecturer at New York University's Center for Management at the School of Continuing and Professional Studies, David was integral in the development of a complete coaching curriculum, and personally teaches a program on how to introduce coaching into large organizations. He is also a casual lecturer at several other universities outside the United States.

David's areas of personal research include the nexus between leadership development and the brain, the impact of a brain-based coaching approach on performance, and how organizations can transform culture through the strategic application of coaching models.

David is a regular speaker at international conferences across the fields of leadership development, talent management, human resources, training, psychology, and coaching. He is also the author of *Personal Best,* published in 2001, and is currently completing *Foundations to Coaching,* a textbook on the science of coaching.

For more information on David's work, see: www.quietleadership.com.

DONE
PG